THE VERMONT LOCAL FOODS

Many stores feature local food products - look for them.

ACKNOWLEDGMENTS

—ᴍᴜ—

Technical assistance by Kathy Callan-Rhondeau & Kathleen Fallon
Recipe testing and tasting by John Greenall & a lot of dinner guests
Many thanks to those that contributed their special recipes

Cover photo by Sue Greenall
(Pear compote with wild orchard pears)

Vermonters' Guide to Gathering, Growing and Cooking Local Foods
Copyright 2009 by Susan Greenall
Third printing
All Rights Reserved

Printed in the United State of America
Printed by R.C. Brayshaw & Company, Inc
ISBN# 978-1-4276-3965-3

Vermont backyard sugarin'

For additional copies
Greenall@vermontel.net
www.vermontel.com/~greenall

THE VERMONTERS' PATH TO LOCAL FOODS

When the White House announced it would be putting in a vegetable garden, the first since Eleanor Roosevelt's Victory Garden, and growing a lot of their own food, Vermont took notice. A local sustainability group in Montpelier went to work on obtaining permission to put a community garden on the State House lawn. The purpose of the garden was to inspire Vermonters to grow their own food and teach them how. Montpelier now boasts a bountiful garden.

The bounty of Vermont is amazing. Not only does the land produce wild foods for gathering but the variety which small farmers offer, from free-range chickens to raw milk cheeses, makes for some great eating. Weekly farmer's markets are proof of the healthy concepts adopted by local food producers for which we all benefit; dollars spent locally, stay local.

The town of Brattleboro, Vermont, holds it's annual "Strolling of the Heifers," a weekend full of cows, kids and local foods, to promote local agriculture. Other towns put the emphasis on "back to basics" into their "Old Home Days" events. The local food movement has hit its stride with seed, seedling and poultry purchases increasing in an otherwise decreasing economy. Not just Vermonters, it appears many Americans are going back to the basics.

This cookbook puts forth a challenge, not only to eat locally and eat healthy, but to eat "outside the box;" changing familiar recipes to conform to using local products, reviving historic recipes, and creating completely new recipes to celebrate awareness of the environment. I included only a few recipes per food, the idea to stimulate the creativity of the cook to modify further recipes and to go exploring for new and exciting food sources.

The challenge is in shifting one's buying and eating habits to reflect products in season and letting them go until that season rolls around again. World wide markets have led us to reach for an apple or tomato or ear of corn any time we want. One can only hope that we have noticed that those apples, tomatoes and ears of corn are but a shadow of those items when in season locally. Not to mention the carbon footprint of an ear of corn in a Vermont produce section in February.

The term localvore was coined as a way to explain one's commitment to only eating food grown within a 100-mile radius and has become increasingly fashionable, but not easy, as it leaves out sugar, spices and coffee. A more realistic term, eating locally, will bring you to look forward to seasonal foods and snubbing the globally marketed facsimiles.

This cookbook is set up by food items. Mainly because when they are season, you should be trying out as many great recipes as you can. Then move onto the next food item. And the next. This will take you through the seasons and have you looking for ramps and fiddleheads in the spring, gathering berries all summer and marveling at what great dishes can come from your freezer, root cellar or pantry in the winter.

In addition to locally found food recipes, some very interesting historical recipes have been included. Some are long forgotten but well worth resurrecting, such as the pear upside down spice cake. I got into a little trouble with using only local ingredients however. Seems that the Connecticut River was a pipeline for items such as oysters, spices and pineapples from Boston harbored ships. A telegraph to Boston in the morning would produce fresh oysters for dinner. Hardly local, but tell the settlers that!

So I have made some concessions for historical recipes, some of which were handed down from the far away roots of settlers and definitely have a foreign ring to them. But there are also the true Vermont recipes, such as dried applesauce and sugar on snow.

The end result of reading through this cookbook should have you marking out where thimble berries bloom so you can return in the

—〰—

WHAT CAN YOU USE?
HARD TO DO WITHOUT, NON-LOCAL INGREDIENTS

Barbara Kingsolver, who wrote "Animal, Vegetable, Miracle" and lived the life of a localvore for a year, allowed each member of her family one luxury item that came from far away. Her husband chose coffee, her children chocolate, and spices were her indulgence. It was a good idea and one to consider. Some solace can be had by buying only Vermont processed or packaged items, such as coffee , balsamic vinegar and flour. Most people have trouble eating a totally local diet although it is an interesting exercise. More pragmatic is eating foods in season and substituting with local ingredients when you can. Thanks to increasing awareness of where food comes from by consumers, local farms that cater to their needs have increased by 20% and eating locally is easier than it was even five years ago.

Sugar - Columbus picked up sugar cane in the islands and by the 1700's it was traded throughout the world. While New Englanders had maple syrup sugar and honey, cane sugar was readily available to them, which might make you feel better when using it.

Confectioners sugar is simply finely ground cane sugar with a bit of corn starch.

Brown sugar – Cane sugar with 3-6% molasses added. It was widely used by the settlers in recipes. It could be made by adding 1 ½ T molasses to 1 cup of cane sugar.

Olive oil – Distinct in taste, it is critical to some recipes.

Pepper – The dried fruit of a vine or tree that does not grow in Vermont or anywhere near Vermont.

Salt – Salt is perhaps the oldest traded good known to man. Short of boiling down several gallons of sea water (which means a trip to the coast) to get a cup of salt, there is no substitute.

Spices - The Connecticut River allowed for the transport of spices to even the most remote Vermont settlers. Boston harbor and Bath, Maine, were bustling with trade from the Indies making spices such as cinnamon, nutmeg, cloves, allspice and ginger commonplace ingredients in Vermont cooking. Certainly not local, one could avoid recipes using them, or not.

HOME-MADE INGREDIENTS

The following items could be made at home, some easier than others. The main thing to consider is that it takes a year to supply your pantry with such items. You can't start making apple cider vinegar in May, you need to wait until apple season and then wait for the cider to ferment. Happily, some of these products are made and sold locally.

Apple Cider Vinegar - One of the mistakes when making hard cider was apple cider vinegar. In order for cider to ferment to produce alcohol, the desired result, the liquid had to be kept away from oxygen. This was done by placing the cider in large wooden barrels and sealing them while they fermented. Should air leak in, the result was vinegar. Naturally fermented vinegar develops a "mother", a cloudy substance made of bacteria and yeast cells that have died, when the alcohol is converted to vinegar in the presence of oxygen. However, apple cider vinegar was very useful in cooking and was considered healthy to drink. Apple cider vinegar, complete with the mother, is available in stores.

Baking Soda - Although baking powder, or sodium bicarbonate, is a naturally occurring substance, the first process for actually making it was developed nearly 150 years ago and sold throughout the world. It eventually found its way into Vermont kitchens along with salt and sugar. There was a process to make baking soda from potash, at one time a big product of Vermont, but it was long and laborious. When baking soda is combined with moisture and an acidic ingredient, the resulting chemical reaction produces bubbles of carbon dioxide that expand causing baked goods to rise.

Baking Powder - Baking powder contains sodium bicarbonate and an acidifying agent, cream of tartar, and also a drying agent, usually starch. Mass production of baking powder started in 1898. Double-acting powder works in two phases, some gas is released when the powder is added to dough, but the majority of the gas is released after the temperature of the dough increases in the oven.

Beer – There is no lack of microbreweries in Vermont although not always made from Vermont grown products.

Bread crumbs – Place any bread pieces not used or getting old into a bag and freeze. When you get enough, run the frozen pieces through a food processor until fine and then refreeze.

Beef broth – Any leftover meat and bones make a wonderful broth. Vegetables or vegetable peelings can be added to add depth to the flavor. Strain and freeze until needed.

Chicken broth – Any leftover chicken or bones can be boiled, strained and frozen until needed. The bones, especially, add a rich flavor to the broth.

Fats and Oils - Early settlers used "drippings", fat from meats, and butter to cook with as well as lard rendered from pigs. Today this is not a good health choice. The only local option is sunflower oil which is grown and made in Vermont.

Mayonnaise - A rather new condiment compared to many others, mayonnaise was not commercially available until 1905. It is easily made in a blender from local ingredients and it much more flavorful.

1 egg
1 t prepared mustard
1 t honey or maple syrup
½ t salt
3 T cider vinegar
1 c sunflower oil

Combine in a blender and slowly drizzle in the oil until thick. Refrigerate.

Mustard
You can make your own from wild or cultivated mustard plants, lots of recipes available, or avail yourself of the incredible variety of mustards made in Vermont and offered in stores.

Pectin – A naturally occurring substance found in fruits that acts as a gelling agent for jams and jellies. Apples, quince and plums contain a lot of pectin, berries and rosehips very little. Before 1825, home cooks extracted pectin from somewhat green apples by boiling them similar to making applesauce and then collecting the clear drippings when put through cheese cloth. It can be canned or frozen for later use.

Vegetable broth – Any liquid from cooking any vegetable is valuable for its flavor and nutrients. Add to it peelings from any vegetable, especially potatoes, boiled for a hour, then strain . Pour into a container and keep in the freezer until needed. Water used to boil eggs, which contains calcium, and can be added to this broth.

Wine – The Champlain Valley offers some excellent wine choices.

Yeast -Before yeast was available in grocery stores, bakers kept colonies of yeast for making bread, known as starters.. You can make your own starter using commercial yeast or by using water from boiled potatoes to attract and feed wild yeasts present in the air or cultivate the white powder, yeast, on wild or organic grapes. Over time, the yeast's natural fermentation process will develop wonderful flavors, giving you a one-of-a-kind family heirloom. If you plan on using yeast a lot for baking, search for bulk quantities of yeast, rather than the packets, which is far more economical.

APPLES

If my horses know anything about apples, they certainly can tell store bought from locally grown. Offer them anything but a local apple when in season and they will turn up their noses. Johnny "Appleseed" Chapman gets the credit for carrying the apple to places where it had never been before. A native fruit of Kazakhstan (where? A former Russian province on the Caspian Sea), the apple was developed and grafted by the Chinese. The apple that came to the New World had been worked over by civilization for centuries. What Johnny Appleseed did was unique, he started all over by growing plants from seeds. This allowed new varieties, by the thousands, to develop. Sadly, only a handful of selected varieties are known to us today, products of grafting to produce a fruit that looks pretty and stores well, not necessarily taste good. Vermont apple trees, some over 150 years old, offer us those unique apples that earned their place for flavor. Amazingly, these forgotten varieties of apples seem to thrive and produce fruit with no help from man. OK, they have some bumps and marks on them, but compare them with the heavily sprayed, spiffed and polished apple found in the store and they hold their own, especially for baking. If you find yourself without a Vermont apple tree, make friends with someone who does. Apples will mature with cool weather and sweeten with a frost. Usually such trees haven't been pruned in a decade or three so picking may necessitate an apple picker, although the windfalls are just as good. The ones you don't use, give to the horses, they love them.

APPLE PAN DOWDY

There is an old colonial song about Pandowdy;
>...*the turkey's in the pan*
>*and the dowdy's on the fire*
>*and we're all getting ready for Cousin Jedediah*
>*and Nehemiah*
>*and Hezekiah*
>*Oh won't we have a jolly time*
>*We'll all take tea*

Tea, of course, was the real treat after the Revolutionary war.

Or there was the 1946 song by Dinah Shore;

If you wanna do right by your appetite,
If you're fussy about your food,
Take a choo-choo today, head New England way,
And we'll put you in the happiest mood. with:
Shoo Fly Pie and Apple Pan Dowdy
Makes your eyes light up,
Your tummy say "Howdy."
Shoo Fly Pie and Apple Pan Dowdy
I never get enough of that wonderful stuff.

Apple Pan Dowdy is without a doubt a traditional Vermont treat.

¼ **pound butter**
1/2 - 1 cup light brown sugar (adjust to sweetness of apples)
¼ **t cinnamon**
¼ **t nutmeg**
1/8 t cloves
5-8 tart apples, pared and cut into eighths

Crust
1 cup flour
2 t baking powder
1 ½ T butter
1/3 cup milk

Melt the butter in a deep ovenproof dish. Add 1 cup sugar and the
seasonings and mix well. Add the apples and toss in the mixture.
Put the dish in the oven at 450 degrees and bake until the apples start
to soften and the syrup is bubbling up amount them, about 10-15
minutes depending on the variety of apple. In the meantime, make
the dough. Mix the flour and baking powder, cut in the butter with
a pastry knife until it is in very small lumps. Cut in the milk. Toss
the dough on a very lightly floured board, kneed it briefly and pat or
roll it out to about ¾ of an inch thick. Cut into 2" squares. When the
apples are bubbling, take the dough and place the squares over the
apples leaving little spaces between each piece. The heat from the
apples is necessary to make the biscuit crust rise. Return to the oven
and reduce the heat to 400 degrees until the top is puffed and well
browned, about 15 minutes.

"QUIET EYE ELMER" APPLESAUCE

From 1950 to 1999, Elmer Phillips ran an apple orchard in Pomfret, VT. In addition, well into his 80's, he wrote a weekly column on all kinds of topics, including apples, for the Vermont Standard. This is his "secret" recipe for pink applesauce.

6 quarts of Vermont apples, cored and quartered, NOT peeled.
1 cup apple cider
¼ cup maple syrup
1 stick cinnamon
½ of a whole nutmeg

Cook the apples in their skins (the secret!) until soft, about 20 minutes. Run through a Foley mill. The applesauce will be pink. Serve warm or cold.
From the kitchen of Elmer Phillips

APPLES A LA VERMONT

4-6 Vermont local apples
¼ cup hard cider
4 T sugar
2 T butter
1/3 cup maple syrup, darker is better
3 T Vermont apple brandy
Vermont vanilla ice cream

Preheat broiler. Peel, core and cut apples into fat ¼-inch thick slices, cover with cider and half the sugar. Place the butter in a shallow baking pan in the warm oven to melt. Place the apples on the coated surface in a single layer and broil approximately 6 inches from the flames until the apples are golden, about 7 to 10 minutes. Sprinkle on remaining sugar and broil until the edges are just beginning to darken or slightly char. Meanwhile bring the maple syrup to a boil in a deep pot, being careful as it will tend to froth, adding the brandy after 3 minutes. Serve hot apples with the sauce accompanied by Vermont vanilla ice cream.

BAKED APPLES

Baked apples are best done in an apple baker, a small ceramic or porcelain bowl with a distinctive center post where the cored apple is place upside down. The bowl helps cook the apple from the inside out and the result is delightful. Microwaves can also be used to bake apples but take care as the cooking time varies greatly with varieties of apples and you could end up with applesauce.

When coring the apple, leave the bottom intact so you can stuff it later. You may want to peel the skin off from the top half for easier eating. While the apple is baking, mix together your choice of;
Dried currents
Dried cranberries
Maple syrup
Honey
Sunflower seeds
Spoon the filling into the cored apple and serve with local vanilla ice cream or whipped cream.

CIDER AND ITS PRODUCTS

Apples were not so much eaten in the past as they were turned into cider. The term "hard" cider is redundant, all cider was hard. Vermont was loaded with apple mills, huge, water driven presses where wagonloads of apples were taken to be processed. The cider was then stored in large wooden barrels in the cellar and everyone, even the kids, drank it. Somewhat by accident it was discovered that cider, left out in minus 20 degrees, pours off as 80 proof applejack. In 1810, Vermont produced over 173,000 gallons of apple brandy. No wonder every Vermont farm had an orchard!

Sweet cider - Take a bunch of windfall apples, put them through a cider press and you have sweet cider. Commercial cider contains a preservative to keep it from becoming hard cider. Sweet cider keeps well frozen.

Hard cider – Left on its own, cider will ferment from the yeast and bacteria on the skins and become an alcoholic beverage weaker than beer, about 3%. The bacteria cannot always be trusted so a "starter" is often added. Vermont rule of thumb is to leave that fall's crop to sit until the first full moon in March. The end result is a dry, somewhat acidic beverage that I like to use as a substitute for lemon juice. To get the bubbly product you see bottled and sold, a second fermentation is needed. The cider is bottled with sugar or maple syrup added and allowed to ferment further producing a carbonated beverage with about 6% alcohol.

Applejack – This smooth, dry liquor with a slight apple taste is uniquely delicious. It is commercially made from a recipe handed down from George Washington. Vermonters made their own on a cold, minus 20 degree night by allowing hard cider to freeze. The alcohol does not freeze and is squeezed out from the frozen mush.

Apple brandy - Or Pomme du Vie, locally produced and delicious.

Apple cider vinegar – First you make the cider, then you let it ferment into alcohol, then you allow the alcohol to convert to acetic acid and then you have vinegar. This happened on its own in the cider barrels in the cellar as the hard cider was drawn off and the contents came into contact with air. By the time one got to the bottom of the barrel, it was vinegar and no longer good to drink. Hence the saying, "bottom of the barrel," meaning, no good.

It takes two good men to press cider.

BEANS - DRIED

Early New Englanders traveling north to Vermont carried a checnk of beans, frozen string and all, hanging from the sides of their oxcarts. Stopping for dinner, it was melted over a fire in an iron kettle to which the beans were added and brown bread laid over the top. The covered kettle soon produced a hearty meal. From that simple recipe arouse countless ways to cook beans. Cooking in a brick oven was the norm, however it required the knowledge of placing an exact fire and the ability to handle a long-handled iron shovel called a peel. Native Americans originated "bean hole beans" by baking beans with bear grease and maple syrup in clay pots covered with deerskins and buried in coals in the ground. Vermonters modified this process with the traditional bean hole a stone-lined pit in which a fire is built until a good bed of coals forms. A cast iron bean pot is lowered into the pit, covered with soil and allowed to cook overnight. In July, at Old Home Days in South Royalton, Vt., Paul and Marion Whitney have been serving up "bean hole beans" for over 40 years.

There are many kinds of beans

Soldier – white elongated beans with a red spot, an heirloom dating pre-1800's.

Yellow-eye – are white with a big light brown spot around the eye. They date back to 1860's in New England, used for "Boston Baked Beans."

Navy (pea) – small white round beans.

Great Northern – Dating back to 1907, a white bean similar to the navy bean.

Jacobs cattle –a sweet bean with maroon and white markings and an old New England favorite.

Kidney – brick red and shaped like a kidney.

Marfax – a golden brown bean that has been New England favorite for generations.

Black turtle – a jet black heirloom bean dating back to the 1700's.

True Red Cranberry – a Maine heirloom favorite of lumberjacks. Deep red, like a cranberry.

Mayflower – brought over in 1620 and certainly a dish at the first Thanksgiving. Delicious but has strings.

"Full of beans" – *In good form or condition; as full of health,*
spirits, or capacity as a horse after a good feed of beans.

VERMONT BAKED BEAN SUPPER

Across New England a tradition of baked bean suppers takes place in community institutions such as churches, granges, and firehouses. The tradition of baked beans for Saturday night supper seems to have originated with the Pilgrims, who would cook enough so that they would not have to cook on the Sabbath. The eating of beans extends to Sunday morning as well, and many Mainiacs speak of eating beans for Sunday morning breakfast. Today, bean suppers are often used as fund-raisers. My friend's mother asks us to make "end of the run" maple syrup, which is very dark with a slight bitter taste, for her baked beans and we have found this to be a suitable substitute for molasses.

4 cups yellow-eye beans
1 pound salt pork
2 small onions
1 t mustard
4 T maple syrup (the darker the better)

Soak the beans overnight. Drain in the morning, cover with cold water and heat slowly by keeping the water just under the boiling point for about 40 minutes. Beans are tested by spooning out a few and blowing on them gently, the skin will crack. Drain off the beans and save the water. Cut a thin slice of the pork and place it on the bottom of the bean pot (there is the Boston Bean pot, brown and white and made of stoneware and the cast iron bean pot with little feet to prevent the bottom from burning). Put the onions in whole (they will vanish in the cooking). Put some beans on top of the onions. Make several gashes an inch deep in the remaining pork rind and place it into the pot. Surround it with the remainder of beans letting the rind show on top. Mix the mustard and maple syrup with a cup of boiling water and pour to cover the beans (you may need to add more water). Put the lid on the bean pot and set it into a slow oven, 300 degrees, for 8 hours. You may need to add more water occasionally. For the last hour, uncover the beans so the pork rid will brown.

Served with Boston Brown or Rye 'n Injin' Bread ⇢ ⇢

BOSTON BROWN BREAD
(A must with baked beans in Boston)

½ cup flour
¾ cup sugar
1 ½ t salt
½ t baking soda
½ cup corn meal
3 cups whole wheat flour
¾ cup dark molasses
1 egg
2 cups milk
1/2 cup melted butter

Sift flour, baking soda, sugar, and salt together. Mix in corn meal and whole wheat flour. Add remaining ingredients, mixing only until all of the flour is moistened. Pour into 2 greased 9x5x3 inch loaf pans. Bake at 300 degrees for 1 hour and 15 minutes. Remove from pans and cool. (Slice with a string – butter it and run it briefly under the broiler and then use to cut)

RYE AND INJIN'
(A must with baked beans for some Vermonters)

Drippings for greasing (fat from cooking beef or pork)
1 ½ cup cornmeal
1 ½ cup rye flour
2 t baking soda
2 eggs
1 t salt
1 cup buttermilk
¾ cup molasses

Arrange 2 racks in oven. On the low one place a baking pan and fill with hot water. Heat oven to 200 degrees. Generously grease other pan with drippings. In large bowl mix well: meal, flour, baking soda and salt. In small bowl beat eggs; stir in milk, then molasses. Pour liquid into dry and stir just until moistened. Do not over beat. Pour batter into pan and smooth out. Cover with a baking sheet. Place on top rack directly above water. Bake 12 hours. (It will be ready after 4, but the old-timers seemed to feel "the longer the better".)

BEEF

The Vermont Beef Producers Association is a wealth of information on where to find local, grass-raised beef. The demand for local beef is increasing by 40% a year and Vermont currently has over 1,000 non-dairy beef producers. Along with the usual Angus and Hereford herds there are heritage or rare breeds such as Scottish Highland, Devon , Galloway, and Miniature Lowline Cattle. There are even beefalo and water buffalo raised for meat in Vermont. You can reserve a side of beef or just buy the cuts that you want. Many Vermont stores carry local beef as do farmer's markets making it easier and easier to acquire. Prior to the Civil War, a steak was not a common part of an American's diet. A side of beef was often hung against a cold wall in the house where it froze and pieces were cut off as needed. Smoking and curing was the only other way of preserving meats and methods differed greatly, from elaborate smoke houses to hanging the meat from the house rafters and allowing the smoke from the fire do the work. Grass-fed beef will have less fat and should be cooked rare to medium and will require 30% less cooking time. Prepare the meat for cooking at room temperature, not chilled. The next time you dine out in a restaurant in Vermont, compliment the chef if local, grass-fed beef is on the menu.

BEEF KABOBS ON THE GRILL

1/2 pounds boneless beef top sirloin steak, cut 1 inch thick
2 t black pepper
3/4 t salt
2 cloves garlic, minced
Green or red pepper and onion slices can be added if desired.

Sauce:
1 T butter
1 medium onion, finely chopped
4 cloves garlic, minced
2 roasted red peppers, rinsed, drained, finely chopped
1/2 cup dry white wine
2 T tomato paste
3/4 t dried thyme leaves, crushed or 2 t minced fresh thyme
1 cup beef broth
4 t flour

Heat the butter in a large skillet over medium heat, add the onion and garlic and cook until tender. Add the pepper, wine, tomato paste and herb of choice. Stir to blend. Combine the broth with the flour in a small bowl and add to the skillet mixture, bringing to a boil. Reduce, stir and simmer for 10 -15 minutes until thickened. Remove from the heat and keep warm. Cut the beef into 1 ¼ inch cubes. Mix the salt, pepper and 1 clove of garlic in a bowl and toss in the beef to coat. Thread the pieces on metal skewers, leaving a small space between each, and grill about 7-10 minutes, turning once.
If adding peppers and onion, par boil the pieces before placing on the skewers.
Serve with dipping sauce.

YANKEE POT ROAST

As with any historic regional dish, there is no single "correct" recipe for Yankee Pot Roast, and each family's recipe was considered the best. What makes this dish unique is the combination or braising and roasting the meat. This probably arose from the necessity to make a good meal from less expensive cuts of meat. True to Yankee practicality, vegetables appearing in the recipe depend upon what is available and economical, most commonly onions, potatoes and carrots, but turnips, parsnips and even celeriac can be used.

Chuck roast, 4- 5 pounds, trimmed of excess fat
Salt and pepper
Sunflower oil
4-5 cloves garlic, sliced
1 large carrot, chopped
1 onion, chopped
1 celery stalk, chopped
2 t dried thyme or 6 sprigs fresh
2 bay leaves
3 T flour
3 ½ cups water or 1/2 chicken stock, 1/2 water. Do not use beef stock.
2 T tomato paste
8 – 10 small onions
5 carrots in 1 -2 inch pieces
1 pound red potatoes or larger white potatoes in chunks

Over high heat, pour oil to cover the bottom of a large heavy pot that will fit in your oven. Generously salt and pepper both sides of the roast and sear meat until well browned on both sides. Remove meat and pour off oil. On medium heat, add chopped carrot, celery, onion and the garlic. Cook adding a small amount of oil if needed until softened but not browned. Sprinkle flour over vegetables and stir for 2-3 minutes. Return meat, adding water, tomato paste and herbs. Bring to a simmer on top of the stove and cover tightly. Place into preheated 325 degree oven and cook for 2 hours. Check at 1 hour and turn meat. Add additional water to keep the meat covered and the consistency of thin gravy. At 2 – 2 ¼ hours, add remaining vegetables. Cook for a total of 3 hours. If the vegetables are not quite cooked, cover and let sit as cooking will continue using retained heat. Season to taste.

NEW ENGLAND BOILED DINNER & ⇢

What makes this dish unique is the use of grey-cured brisket of beef, parsnips and beets. There are other variations of boiled dinners, such as Ireland's corn beef and cabbage, but New England put its stamp on this dish through the way the brisket is cured. Gray curing is a regional specialty and uses no chemical preservatives. Not everyone likes this dish but it is unique and speaks of a time when world wide cuisine did not exist. This is a hearty meal for large winter gatherings.

1 5-6 pound grey cured brisket of beef
6-10 beets
20 small boiling onions
6-8 carrots
6-8 potatoes
6 small purple topped turnips
6 parsnips, peeled
1 small head of savory cabbage, cut in wedges
2 T parsley
Horse radish sauce
Bouquet Garni
3 bay leaves
1 T whole black peppercorns
5-6 sprigs of thyme
1 t mustard seed
1-2 dried chile peppers

Tie up in a piece of cheesecloth and leave a long string. Using a very large pot, cover the brisket by several inches of water, bring to a boil and simmer, skimming off the top fat. Add the bouquet garni and tie the end of the string on the pot handle for easy removal. Simmer for 3 hours, checking after 2 hours with a large fork. When done the fork should pierce the meat easily. In the meantime, scrub and cook the beets until tender, rinse in cold water and peel off the skins and keep warm. When the meat is tender, add the onions, carrots, potatoes, turnips and parsnips. Simmer for another 20 minutes then remove the brisket and keep it warm. Return the pot to a boil and add the cabbage for 10-15 minutes. Turn off the heat and remove the bouquet garni. Carve the meat and place on a very large platter. Arrange the vegetables, including the beets, around the meat and sprinkle with the parsley. Serve with horse radish sauce on the side.

RED FLANNEL HASH

Leftovers from the New England Boiled Dinner are used for the next morning's breakfast hash. The red color comes from the beets.

2 cups boiled beef
1 cup cooked vegetables
2-3 cups cooked potatoes
1 cup cooked beets
1/3 to ½ cup broth from the dinner
2-4 slices of bacon (for the fat)
Chopped scallions or parsley
1 egg per person

Chop the leftover meat and vegetables and mix them together in a bowl. Add the scallions or parsley. Heat the bacon in a skillet until it starts to release some fat. Spoon in the meat and vegetable mixture and pat it down to cover the bottom of the skillet. Pour in 1/3 cup of the broth, cooking until a crisp brown crust forms, 20-30 minutes, adding more broth if it starts to get too dry. Fold the hash over like an omelet. Place a poached egg on top and serve immediately

With two meals like this, back to back, you will need to cut and stack a cord of wood to work it off. I suppose that was the idea back then.

BEETS

Even if you don't like beets, they are worth planting in the garden for their tender young greens. Beet greens add color and flavor to any garden salad and can be harvested until frost. Beets are a colorful and tasty addition, hot or cold, to any meal. Beets are an integral part of the traditional New England Dinner and the colorful part of Red Flannel Hash made from the leftovers of that dinner.

BAKE, BOIL OR GRATE

Wash and trim off the tops and roots but no need to peel. Place beets in a roasting pan, add a little water for steam and cover with foil or a lid. Roast the beets at 425 degrees for 30-45 minutes or until the beets are easily pierced with a fork. Place in cold water and allow to cool until you can slip off the skins. If boiling, cook for 20-30 minutes until tender, place in cold water and slip off the skins. You can now do all kinds of things with your cooked beets.

Slice, dice or shred and add to a green salad or as a side to sandwiches or salads.

Toss with
2 T **oil**
1 T **balsamic vinegar**
salt and pepper
herb of choice (anise is nice), minced.
Serve hot or cold.

In a medium sauté pan, melt
2 T butter and mix in
1 T honey and **1 T cider vinegar** until warm.
Toss in the cooked beets and coat with the mixture. Serve hot or cold.

BEET AND BEET GREEN SALAD

4 large beets
1/4 cup pumpkin seeds, toasted
1 bunch beet greens

2 scallions, finely chopped
1/4 lb feta cheese (optional)
Dressing
3 T olive oil
2 T balsamic vinegar
¾ t mustard
1 t pepper
1 T basil leaves, finely chopped

Remove the greens from the beets and rinse in cold water. Bake or boil the beets, remove the skins. Fill a large skillet with water to a depth of 1 inch and heat to a simmer and drop in the greens. Let them cook for about 30 seconds, until tender and juicy. Place greens in a colander and gently run cold water over them to halt cooking. Whisk together all dressing ingredients. Slice beets. Squeeze excess water out of the cooked beet greens and chop. Put beets, beet greens, pumpkin seeds, and scallions in a salad bowl. Pour dressing over salad and toss gently. Crumble feta cheese on top. Serve at room temperature or chilled.

Also see -New England Boiled Dinner & Red Flannel Hash

VERMONT FARMER'S MARKETS

Barre City, Farmers Market, Barre, VT
Bellows Falls Farmers' Market Bellows Falls, VT
Bethel Farmers Market Bethel, VT
Bradford Farmer's Market Bradford, VT
Brattleboro Area Farmers' Market Brattleboro, VT
Charlotte Farmers Market, Charlotte, VT
Chelsea Farmers' Market Chelsea, VT
Chester Farmers' Market Chester, VT
The Farmer and The Flea Ascutney, VT
Groton Growers Market Groton, VT
Mount Tom Farmers' Market Woodstock, VT
Norwich Farmers' Market Norwich, VT
Randolph Farmers' Market Randolph, VT
Royalton Farmers' Market South Royalton, VT
Stowe Farmers Market, Stowe, VT
Townshend Common Farmers' Market Townshend, VT
Washington Village Farmers Market Washington, VT
West River Farmer's Market Londonderry, VT
Windsor Farmers' Market Windsor, VT
Woodstock Market on the Green Woodstock, VT

BERRIES

If you are gathering wild berries, please ask permission of the landowner first.

Strawberries - You don't have to go looking for wild strawberries, they will find you. Just don't mow part of your lawn and the strawberry plants will reveal themselves by their blooms. They are ripe when a stroll across that lawn releases the delicious aroma of stomped fruit! June/July

Blueberries - Not just grown in Maine, blueberries do very well in Vermont and will produce from late July through September.

Red Raspberries - Cultivated bushes do very well in Vermont, some varieties producing twice, once in July and again in October. The wild variety is harder to come by but exquisite in flavor.

Black Raspberries - These prolific berry bushes can be found just about anywhere. While they look like a black version of a red raspberry, they have a different texture and taste. In July one could practically dine on a good stand of black raspberry bushes. Best picked daily for freshness.

Blackberries - Another prolific berry, these will start to ripen in late August and go into October. Somewhat more fickle than black raspberries as weather conditions must be ideal for a good crop. Otherwise a promising crop of berries can dry up in hot, dry weather.

Thimble berries - The gourmet of Vermont berries, these lovely ruby red berries are the last to ripen but well worth waiting for. Named such as they resemble a thimble when picked. Never commercialized due to being rather delicate to handle, picked in the wild and brought to the table they are outstanding. The thornless bushes grow along streams with the leaves looking somewhat grape like. The best way to locate thimble berries is to make note of the pretty pink blooms and come back to harvest the berries which "hide" under the leaves. Unripe berries are white and the plant will ripen berries over a 6-10 week period from mid-August until frost. The berries can be frozen and jam made at a later date.

20

BERRY SOUP

Any **berry** will do
Plain yogurt
Honey
Apple cider, the sweeter, the better
Grated nutmeg

Fresh or frozen cider can be used, always taste and adjust the honey for sweetness. Whisk the yogurt, honey and cider together. Chill thoroughly. Add berries and nutmeg just before serving.

BERRY TARTLETS

Any **berry** will do
Sugar
Pie dough for 2 crusts
Muffin pan, buttered.

Make the pie dough. Roll it out and cut squares slightly larger than the size of each hole in the muffin pan. Lay the dough in the hole, fill with berries and cover with the ends of the dough. Sprinkle with sugar. Bake for 20-30 minutes until dough has started to brown. Pop out the tartlets and serve warm.

BERRY JAM

My new neighbors moved to Vermont from New Jersey because they wanted a change of lifestyle. They embraced everything they laid their eyes on, from waving to everyone they passed while driving (try that in NJ!) to living off the land. Finding herself with a very prolific raspberry patch put in by the previous owner, the challenge was what to do with them all. Jam! Buckets of raspberries and days later, this recipe was perfected. It was so good that it was entered in the Tunbridge World's Fair (the oldest fair in the country) where it won first prize. Her secret was to pick fresh berries and simply follow the directions on the back of the pectin box!

Also See -
Chicken with Raspberries
Jellies & Jams
Plum Clafouti

21

BEVERAGES FROM THE GARDEN

RHUBARB DELIGHT

Bring 3 cups of water to a boil
1/3 cup honey or to taste
Add 1 cup rhubarb cut into cubes
When the pot comes to a boil, turn off, add the rhubarb and honey, cover and let it sit for several hours or overnight. Serve cold. The drink is a delightful pink and has the taste of lemonade!
From the kitchen of Linda Schneider

LEMON BALM TEA INFUSION

1 cup of freshly cut lemon balm leaves and stems
Put into a 1 quart jar, bruising the leaves to release the flavor
Add 1/4 cup honey
Add boiling water to fill the jar, cap, seep for 20 minutes. Serve hot or cold.
From the kitchen of Linda Schneider

MINT ICED TEA

4-5 sprigs of freshly cut mint leaves and stems
1 large pot of almost boiling water
As the water starts to boil, turn off the heat and drop in the mint sprigs, seep several hours. Pour the entire pot, sprigs and all, into a beverage container and chill. Will keep for 4-5 days and the flavor will age.

MINT HOT TEA

Place **dried mint leaves** in a tea ball in a tea cup and pour hot water over allowing to seep for 5 minutes.

SWITCHEL

You do not need to be making hay on a hot August day to enjoy this old Vermont remedy for hot, sweaty laborers. Occasionally some good old New England rum has found its way into switchel but that was purely accidental.

½ gallon spring water
1/4 cup cider vinegar
3/4 cup maple syrup
1 t powdered ginger
Mix, add water to taste, chill and drink.

CARROTS

The cultivated carrot started out purple, the yellow-orange color a mutation. The distinctively purple Beta Sweet carrot is available in the U.S. as are a great variety of the traditional orange ones. Carrots are pretty easy to grow and actually sweeten some when left in the ground for a frost or two. They can be harvested as needed all summer and fall making them a fresh addition to any meal.

CARROTS IN MINT SAUCE

2 cups carrots, whole, halved or diced depending on carrot size
2 **T butter**
1-2 T honey, to taste
1 T fresh or 2 t dried mint

Boil the carrots in just enough water to cover them. Cook for 15-25 minutes or until easily pierced with a fork. While they are cooking, melt the butter and stir in the honey and mint. Do not overheat. Strain the carrots and pour the mint sauce over them and serve hot.

CARROT PUDDING

A traditional dish served in New England modified to ingredients on hand. It shows up in Canadian cookbooks also, dating back to 1877.

1 Cup brown sugar, 1 cup suit, chopped fine, 1 cup raw potatoes, grated, 1 cup raw carrots, grated, 1 cup raisins, 1 cup currants, 1 teaspoon soda sifted in flour, 1 teaspoon each cinnamon and cloves, flour to make a stiff batter. Steam 3 hours.   *Mrs. Wm. Hawkins*

"Suit" is for suet, pure fat found around the kidneys of cattle. Today it is hard to find anyone that likes suet except at the birdfeeder. This is a delicious dish which can be used for breakfast or as an elegant dessert.

1 T butter
1 cup dark brown sugar
1 cup flour
1 cup fresh breadcrumbs
1 t salt
1 t baking soda
1 t ground cinnamon
1 t ground ginger

1 cup cranberries+
1 cup grated carrot
1 cup grated apple
1 cup grated medium potato
1/2 cup oil

Butter a 6 cup pudding mold or 6 ramekins,. Mix dry ingredients in a mixing bowl. Peel the carrot and grate it. Wash and grate the apple and potato. Add these to the dry ingredients with the oil. Let the mixture sit for 20 minutes. Divide the mixture equally between the ramekins, or press it into the single mold. Cover with wax paper and foil, and hold it in place with string. Put the puddings into a large steamer with water coming halfway up jars and seal with a lid or foil. Bring to a boil, steam for 2 hours. Check regularly for more water if needed but don't let your pot boil dry. +Cranberries are grown in Vermont!

PUDDING SAUCE

There are a lot of variations as to the sauce served on carrot pudding

HARD SAUCE
1/2 cup soft butter
1 1/2 cup sifted confectioners' sugar
2 T Apple brandy or applejack

Cream butter with confectioners' sugar until light and fluffy. Stir in apple brandy or applejack.

HOT PUDDING SAUCE
1 cup sugar
1/2 cup butter
1/2 cup cream

Heat all ingredients in double boiler until well blended. Serve hot.

BROWN SUGAR SAUCE
1 cup brown sugar
2 T cornstarch
1/4 t salt
2 cups warm water
2 T butter
2 t Apple brandy

Combine brown sugar, cornstarch and salt in a saucepan. Add warm water gradually, stirring constantly. Cook and stir over low heat, until thick and smooth, about 3 minutes. Remove from heat, add butter and vanilla. Serve hot.

24

CHEESE

Vermont. Cows. Cheese. Actually not quite that simple but Vermont certainly has grown to be an outstanding cheese producing state. Odds are that there is a farm almost under your nose that makes a variety of wonderful cheeses. Seek them out and start experimenting. Each cheese has its own history and method of how it is made which is fascinating in itself. For example, cheddar cheese is named after a step in its making; cheddaring. This is a multi-step process that gives cheddar its unique flavor. Every ten minutes when the loaves of curd must be turned, they are stacked. The first time, two loaves are stacked together. The next time the loaves are turned, two stacks of two are put together. When the stacks get large enough (generally four high), stacking stops but the loaves are still turned every ten minutes. This process is complete when the acidity of the whey is between .5 and .7, so it is checked constantly. If this step is not done, its not cheddar cheese!

Try making your own! Before the age of pasteurization crème fraîche made itself as the bacteria present in the cream fermented and thickened it naturally. There are wonderful books, even a CD, that will instruct even the most timid of us to make farmhouse cheddar, mozzarella, fromage blanc, whole milk ricotta, creme fraiche and mascarpone.

ARTISAN GRILLED CHEESE SANDWICH

Any kind of **cheese**
Any kind of **bread**
Any addition of
    Sliced apples
    Sliced tomatoes and fresh basil
    Sliced cucumbers
    Diced garlic scapes
    Two or three wild leeks with smoked maple syrup+

Grill under a broiler, in a pan or use a Foreman grill. Experiment. Grilled cheese will never be the same again!

+ Smoked maple syrup is one of the most interesting Vermont tastes that can add volumes to any dish.

VERMONT CHEDDAR CHEESE SOUP

New England cheese soup is a classic traditional dish that can be used as a starter in small quantities or as the main dish. It can be served with chopped ham and bread on the side.

1 medium onion, diced
2 stalks celery
1 carrot, diced
6 T butter
4 T flour
4 cups chicken or vegetable broth
1 cup heavy cream
½ pound cheddar cheese, grated
1 t dry mustard
1 bottle dark beer
Salt and pepper

In a heavy soup pot, cook the onion, celery and carrot in the butter until tender, about 5 minutes. Sprinkle the flour on top, making a roux, and cook for another 5 minutes, stirring constantly. Slowly pour in the broth, ½ a cup at a time, allowing the soup to thicken before adding more. After all of the broth has been added, cook at a low simmer for 45 minutes. The soup should be thick enough to coat a spoon. Strain, pushing through any soft mushy vegetables. Return to a low simmer and add the cream, grated cheese and dry mustard, stirring until the cheese is hot but DO NOT boil. Ever. The cheese will separate out. Use a double boiler to keep the soup hot or reheat it. To add flavor or thin the soup, use the beer. Different kinds of beer will affect the taste, all are good, but a rich dark beer will enhance the cheese flavor. I suggest seasoning with salt and pepper after adding the beer.

CHEDDAR-WHEAT BERRY SALAD

1 ½ cups wheat berries+
6 cups water
5 ounces cheddar cheese
1 cup chopped tomatoes

½ cup corn (fresh or frozen)
1 scallion, green and white parts or 3-5 ramps, chopped

Dressing
¼ cup Dijon mustard
¼ cup pure maple syrup
¼ cup apple cider vinegar
¼ cup olive oil
1 clove garlic
1 t chopped rosemary

In a large saucepan, cover the wheat berries with water, bring to a boil and cook until tender, about an hour. Drain well, spread out on a baking sheet and allow to cool. This step can be done hours or a day ahead. In a large bowl, combine the wheat berries with the cheese, tomatoes, corn, and onion or ramps.
Whisk together all of the dressing ingredients and toss with the salad. Allow the flavors to mix for several hours in the refrigerator.

+wheat berries – are the entire grain of a wheat plant

CHEESE SKEWERS

8 oz of your choice of cheese, herbed cheeses especially good
36 fresh basil leaves
36 cherry or grape tomatoes, red or yellow
Toothpicks

Cut cheese into bite size pieces, about ½ inch cubes. Wrap each cube in a basil leaf, spear onto the toothpick and add the tomato at the end. A great summer treat.

Also see –
Pears on Toast with Melted Brie
Cheese Stuffed Potatoes

CHICKEN

Keeping a few hens for eggs is one thing, raising chickens to eat is another. Before considering becoming a chicken farmer, be aware that free range chicken meat is available at stores. That said, more than one person has not been able to do the deed when it came down to it. One of my neighbors, after two days of failing to get this done, finally called their veterinarian (she wasn't so happy doing it either!). The Joy of Keeping Chickens, by Vermont author, Jennifer Megyesi, outlines poultry farming from her experiences at Fat Rooster Farm and is highly recommended reading.

Buying local might mean seeing names on chicken other than "chicken", such as;

Poussin, a very young bird, 14-18 ounces

Hen, an older female bird sold for stew or soup

Pullet, a young hen yet to lay eggs, sold as a broiler or fryer

Roasters, slightly older, male or female, birds and larger, 6-8 pounds

Capons, a castrated male grown to large sizes, 7-12 pounds, and known for their tender and juicy meat.

Rooster, a mature male,very tough to eat, but excellent as Coq au Vin.

CHICKEN IN THE GARDEN

1 cut up chicken
Butter
1 onion
2-3 cups garlic
Add
Green chili peppers to taste (if you don't like spicy, omit)
2-3 red or green sweet peppers
1 large or 2 medium zucchini or summer squash
1 cup tomatoes
2 cups corn kernels
1 t oregano
1 t basil
2 cups broth or water

28

Brown the chicken first, then add onion and garlic in a large kettle. Add the chili peppers, sweet peppers and squash and sauté. As the mixture becomes dry, add the tomatoes, corn, spices and broth. Simmer 30-40 minutes. Garnish with cilantro
From _Animal, Vegetable, Miracle_ – _great reading_!

SAGE SEASONED CHICKEN (?)

1-2 chicken breasts, skinned, boned, cut into cubes
1 clove of garlic
2 T olive oil
2 cups stewed tomatoes
1 medium onion, diced
3 T fresh sage or 3 t dried sage
½ t sugar
1 cup chicken or vegetable broth
½ cup white wine
1 cup milk or ½ cup light cream

Saute the garlic in 1 T olive oil, add the cubed chicken. Cook only until just tender, do not overcook. Remove and reserve the chicken. Add 1 T olive oil and sauté the onion until tender, add tomatoes, broth and wine and bring to a boil. Reduce the heat, add the sage and sugar and simmer for 45 minutes to allow the flavors to blend. Just before serving, add the milk or cream and the reserved chicken. Heat until warm but do not allow it to boil.

RASPBERRY CHICKEN

1-2 chicken breasts, skinned, boned
2 T oil
2 T butter
2 T chives
1 cup raspberries

Sauce
½ cup cold butter
2 T minced shallots
3 T raspberry vinegar (add several raspberries to apple cider vinegar and allow to stand for 3-4 days in the refrigerator)
1 T water
¼ cup light cream
To make the sauce. Melt 1 T butter in a skillet, add the shallots and

cook until soft. Add the vinegar and water and simmer down to 2 T.
Stir in the cream, season with salt and pepper if you wish. Simmer
again, whisking to prevent burning, until the sauce is reduced to 3 T.
Remove from the heat and set aside. This can be made up to 4 hours
before serving. Heat the butter in a clean skillet and cook the chicken
breasts until brown on both sides. Do not overcook. Remove from
the heat and keep warm. Return the sauce to the stove on low heat.
Whisk in COLD butter, 1 T at a time. The butter should soften but
not liquefy. Add 1/3 of the sauce and 1 T of the chives a warm
plate, place the chicken on top and pour the rest of the sauce on top.
Garnish with 1 T of chives.

CHICKEN BREASTS WITH RADISHES

1-2 chicken breasts, skinned, boned
6 radishes
1 cup apple cider vinegar
½ cup dry white wine
2 t fresh tarragon or ½ t dry tarragon
1 t honey

Cut diagonal slices in the breasts to put the radishes in. Consider
how this will look as a final product. Be creative! Cover the bottom
of a shallow dish with sliced radishes and lay the chicken breasts,
cut side down, on top. Combine the vinegar, wine and honey in a
saucepan and simmer for 2 minutes. Stir and pour over the breasts
and marinate overnight in the refrigerator.
To cook. Broil the chicken breasts, cut side down, until brown. Baste
with the marinate and broil on the cut side for 2 minutes. Remove
and place the sliced radishes in the slits, return to the broiler until
done. Serve hot.

Dinner Guests
When guests ask what item they could bring, suggest
something which is local for THEM that you can't get.

Guests from Maine can bring lobster or clams
Guests from Massachusetts can bring scallops
Guests from Canada can bring ice wine
Guests from Pennsylvania can bring dried corn
Guests from Minnesota can bring wild rice

CONCORD GRAPES

Concord grapes grow very well in Vermont as proven when my husband purchased four plants, planted them at the base of our window arbor and fertilized the lot. Four years later we had our first pie and can hardly keep up. The grapes should be allowed to ripen and sweeten, a tricky business because local raccoons will also be watching the grapes for just the right moment for picking too. As will bats, who take tiny bites from the grapes, but do minimal damage compared to raccoons! Concord grapes are also available at local farmers markets and have even been spotted at grocery stores. These recipes also work with wild grapes.

GRAPE PIE

This pie, like making tomato sauce, takes a lot of time but is well worth it because it can be frozen and used year round. The wonderful smell of it cooking is matched by its taste.

3 cups Concord grapes
1 cup sugar
¼ cup flour
¼ t salt
1 T hard apple cider
1 ½ T melted butter
1 unbaked pastry shell *(see Pie Crust Dough)*
Topping
½ cup flour
¼ cup sugar
1/3 cup softened butter

Slip the skins from the grapes, set aside. Bring 3 cups of the pulp to a boil then simmer for 10-15 minutes. Put through a sieve to remove the seeds. Add the skins. Add flour, sugar, salt, hard cider and butter and pour the mixture into the pastry shell. Mix the topping ingredients and sprinkle over the top. Bake at 400 degrees for 40 minutes. Place a pan on the lower rack for drippings - which indicates that the pie is done. Cool for at least an hour before serving. The unbaked pie may also be frozen, thawed and baked. Or the pie filling can be made, frozen, thawed and placed into a fresh pastry shell and baked.

CONCORD GRAPE KUCHEN
AKA - WE ATE THE SEEDS

In my childhood, we ate the seeds! Seeds to everything; grapes and watermelons included. Many countries prize these seeds as a nutritious part of nature. Roasted watermelon seeds are available by street vendors in some countries. Watermelon seed spitting contests were always a childhood delight. We have taken out the "fun". In America, we have stripped out the seeds of grapes, only to sell expensive grape seed extract in health food stores. Now really, how smart is that!?! Why not just eat the seeds in the first place. Eaten whole, they add good fiber that your body needs to keep the colon clean. Crunched between your teeth, they add the nutrients found in the expensive extract. One of my all time favorite recipes is my mother's Concord Grape Kuchen. I have altered it a bit, but I don't think she will mind. The word "kuchen" means cake in German. The flavor of the Concord grape is very intense. Remember to tell your guests, "Please feel free to eat the seeds."

¼ **cup sugar**
1 ½ **cups flour**
1/3 **cup butter**
1/3 **cup milk**
2 **eggs**
½ **t baking soda**
2 **t baking powder**
½ **t salt**
Topping
4 **cups Concord Grapes**
¼ **cup sugar**
4 **T butter**
1 ½ **t cinnamon**
½ **t nutmeg**

1/3 **cup blackberry jam**
1 **T hot water**

Preheat the oven to 400 degrees. Grease 13"x 9" pan. In a large bowl, mix ingredients for cake. With mixer at low speed, beat until mixture leaves sides of bowl and clings to beaters, constantly scraping bowl. Spread dough into baking dish. Cover top with the Concord Grapes.

In small sauce pan over medium heat, melt butter, stir in ¼ cup sugar, cinnamon and nutmeg. Spoon over the grapes. Bake 30 to 35 minutes. In small bowl, with fork, stir jam with 1 T hot water; brush over hot fruit. Serve warm with ice cream.
From the kitchen of Ruth Hrubo and her daughter, Linda K. Schneider

STUFFED GRAPE LEAVES

Rice in Vermont? Several farms have been experimenting with growing rice and, although not yet available at markets, the prospect is exciting.

40 young large leaves or brined leaves (takes a week!)
2 cups rice, cooked (wheatberries can be substituted)
2 medium onions, diced & sautéed
2 lbs ground beef or lamb sautéed
2 T fresh mint, chopped
1 cups apple cider vinegar
1 cups feta, crumbled

If the leaves are not young you will have to brine them in 1 T of salt to a gallon of water. Pour over the leaves and let sit for a week, stirring several times a day. The leaves will soften to a chewy but edible texture. Young leaves should be boiled for 5 minutes or until they change color.
Combine the stuffing ingredients and drop 1-2 T in each leaf, wrap up like little burritos. Bake in oven, covered, for 1 hour at 350 degrees. Sprinkle with more fresh mint leaves. Serve warm.

ICE WINE

Ice wine was probably discovered by accident in the 1700's and has recently enjoyed resurgence in Canada and now Vermont. It requires a special environment and good timing to make ice wine, a delightfully sweet, super-fresh sauterne tasting dessert wine. The Concord grapes are left on the vines until the temperature drops below 20 degrees for at least a day. The frozen grapes are harvested and quickly processed leaving only the sweetest liquid to be squeezed out. The end product is costly because over half of the grape is lost due to the freezing. But ice wine is well worth it.

CORN

If you grow your own corn, be aware that others beside you are interested in the harvest. A friend in Shelburne checked his ears every day to determine when to pick them. Announcing that the long awaited delight was to be served for dinner, he discovered he was a day late…the squirrels had made off with the entire crop! Seems they had a better sense of when that corn was ready than he did! Locally grown corn is not hard to come by and growers are happy to let you know when they are picking so you can beat the squirrels.

Happily, corn freezes fairly well. The trick is to get fresh cobs and get them processed as quickly as possible. Remember electric knives? If you don't have one, ask your aunt. Use that knife to take off the kernels, put them in freezer bags and pop them in the freezer. That simple. When you thaw the corn out, be prepared for a lot of liquid which you may need to drain off to keep whatever you are making from being too soupy. But save that liquid and use it to make into vegetable broth.

ROASTED CORN ON THE COB

A favorite at the Tunbridge World's Fair (the oldest fair not only in Vermont but in the country), there is always a line at the roasted corn stand. Absolutely the best way to eat corn on the cob.

Freshly picked corn
A large tub of cold water
An open fire with a grill

Drop the entire cob, husk and all, into the tub of cold water and leave about an hour. That gives you time to build a wood fire and have good coals ready. Shake off any excess water from the cob and place it on the grill, turning it with a long fork as each side darkens but not burn. When all sides are dark, peel back the husk and silk and enjoy.

ROASTED CORN SALAD

2 T hard apple cider
1 T cider vinegar
2 T fresh basil, shredded

½ cup sunflower seed oil
¼ t salt
Salad
6 ears of corn cut from the cob (about 3 cups)
2 medium tomatoes, cubed
½ cup thinly sliced radishes
2 scallions, trimmed and chopped
Fresh basil for garnish
Chopped ham or sliced salami (optional)

Preheat the oven for 450. In a mixing bowl, toss the corn kernels with just enough oil to coat them. Place on a roasting sheet in a single layer and roast until they begin to shrivel and turn a little golden 4-6 minutes (or skip this step by using fire roasted corn on the cob and cut the corn from the cob,). Set aside to cool. Whisk all of the dressing ingredients in a small bowl. In a large salad bowl, combine and toss lightly all of the salad ingredients. Pour the dressing on top and toss again. Top with ham or salami on the edge.

CORN CHOWDER

3 T butter
3 medium onions, chopped
5 carrots, cut into ¼ inch slices
5 celery stalk, cut into ¼ inch slices
6 cups of corn removed from the cob (about 1 dozen ears)
3 cups broth, chicken or vegetable
¼ t salt
½ t pepper
2 large red or green bell peppers cut into ½ inch pieces
3 T chopped fresh dill, more for garnish

Melt the butter in a large pot, add the onion, carrots and celery and cook until tender, about 10 minutes. Add the corn and cook until heated, about 2 minutes. Remove 4 cups of the vegetables and puree until smooth, then return it to the pot. Add the broth, salt and pepper and bring to a boil. Add the peppers and simmer for 2 minutes. Add the dill and season to taste. Garnish with more dill. The chowder can be made a day ahead but be sure to chill it thoroughly and reheat just before serving.

INDIAN CORN PUDDING

3 eggs
2 T butter
1 T maple sugar (not syrup)
1 cup sweet milk
2 T flour
1 t salt
2 T finely chopped onion
2 cups corn

Beat the eggs until they are light. Add the milk, seasonings and corn and onion. Pour into a buttered dish and bake at 350 degrees until firm, like a custard, about 1 hour.

Maple sugar can be made by following the directions for making maple sugar candy. I suggest using smaller amounts of syrup and storing the sugar in a sealed jar. It will keep indefinitely.

From Native American Recipes

Valley Food & Farm, a program of **Vital Communities,** provides folks in the greater Upper Valley with a variety of ways to find local foods.

Valley Food & Farm Guide lists farms, restaurants and other businesses selling locally grown and raised foods;
Flavors of the Valley expo, held each April, people meet farmers, taste local farm products and see what chefs do with farm foods;
Tidbits, a biweekly email bulletin, gives timely updates of who is growing what and how to get it. (to subscribe, e-mail debbie@vitalcommunities.org)
The Valley Food & Farm (www.vitalcommunities.org, select VF&F Guide), gives up-to-date information on farmstands, farmers' markets, gifts from farms, classes, on-farm activities and much more.

Contact information:
Vital Communities
104 Railroad Row, White River Junction, VT 05001

CORNMEAL

Cornmeal was made by Native Americans long before the Mayflower sailed. Water driven grist mills served many Vermont colonial communities to grind up dried corn in to corn meal. Vermont grown and processed cornmeal is available as is cornmeal mix for pancakes or muffins.

CORNBREAD OR CORN MUFFINS

Native American cornbread was called "pone." For whatever reason, in America, the difference between Southern cornbread and Northern cornbread is huge. Northern cornbread is more like a cake.

1 ¼ cups ground cornmeal
¾ cup flour
1-4 T sugar, to taste
2 t baking powder
½ t baking soda
½ t salt
2 eggs
2/3 cups milk
2/3 cup buttermilk
2-3 T butter

Preheat the oven to 425 degrees. Grease a 9x9-inch pan or a 12-muffin pan. Whisk the dry ingredients together in a large bowl. In a separate bowl, mix together the eggs, milk and buttermilk. Combine and mix just until moistened. Fold in the butter. Pour the batter into the pan and spread evenly. Bake until a toothpick inserted comes out clean, 10 to 12 minutes in a muffin pan, 20 to 25 minutes in a square pan.

CORNMEAL PANCAKES

1 egg, separated
2 cups buttermilk
2 T sunflower oil
½ cup flour
1 t baking soda
1 t salt
1 t sugar
1 ½ cups cornmeal

Beat egg white until stiff peaks form; set aside. Slightly beat the egg yolk in mixing bowl, blending in buttermilk and oil. Mix together the flour, soda, salt, sugar, and cornmeal; blend into the liquid mixture until smooth. Fold in beaten egg white. Let batter stand for 10 minutes. Bake on hot greased griddle until nicely browned on both sides. These cook a little slower than pancakes.

AUTHENTIC INDIAN PUDDING

Obviously, this recipe was developed after settlers reached Vermont and traded sugar and spices with the native people.

4 cups milk
½ cup cornmeal
¾ cup molasses
1 t salt
1 beaten egg
3 T sugar
¼ cup butter
1 t ginger
½ t cinnamon
½ cup currants

Bring the milk to a boil in the top of a double boiler over high heat. Add the cornmeal slowly and cook while stirring for about 15 minutes, the remove from the heat. Stir in the remaining ingredients and pour into a greased 1 ½ quart baking dish. Bake at 300 degrees for about 2 hours. Serve hot.

Traditionally, it was mixed in a water-soaked leather pouch, then held over a campfire, removing the pouch and wetting it form time to time until the ingredients were cooked. Then it was poured onto a flat hot rock by the fire and baked until done.

From Native American Recipes by the Abenaki Clan of the Hawk, Vermont.

Measuring

T = Tablespoon
t = teaspoon
lb = pound

CUCUMBER

From August to October, cucumbers are abundant. Sadly they don't freeze well so celebrate them while they are in season. No need to peel them like store bought cukes as they have a wax over the skin to help preserve them. Eat garden cukes intact! The cucumber originated in India and has been cultivated for over 3,000 years. In the late 1600's, a number of articles in contemporary health publications stated that uncooked plants brought on summer diseases and should be forbidden to children. The cucumber kept this vile reputation for an inordinate period of time: "fit only for consumption by cows", which some believe is why it gained the name, "cowcumber".

NO-COOK CUCUMBER SOUP

It doesn't get any easier than this.

   1 cucumber
   ½ cup milk
   ½ cup plain yogurt
   Fresh dill to taste
   2-3 mint leaves
   1 T honey

Put it all in a food processor and hit the button. The result will be a frothy soup. Chill thoroughly and serve.

CUCUMBER GARDEN SALAD

   4 cucumbers, thinly sliced
   ½ cup red onion, very thinly sliced
   ¾ cup sour cream
   ¾ cup plain yogurt
   2 cloves garlic, crushed
   4 mint leaves, minced or 1 t dried mint
   ¼ cup parsley, chopped
   ¼ cup scallion greens or 2-4 ramp tops, diced

1-2 t honey
1 cup sunflower seeds

Summer greens
Tomato wedges
Hard boiled egg slices
Carrot sticks
Green or red pepper slices

Whisk together the sour cream and yogurt and add the garlic, mint, parsley, scallion or ramp tops and honey. Taste the red onions for sweetness and flavor. If too strong for your taste, mix together 1T sugar and 1T water to made a thick paste. Toss the onion slices in the paste and allow to sit for 10 minutes. This will draw out some of the strong onion taste. Rinse and use. Toss the cucumbers and onions in the dressing and top with sunflower seeds. Chill thoroughly to allow the flavors to blend. Place on a bed of fresh greens and garnish with tomatoes, eggs, carrot sticks, pepper slices, a vegetable of your choice or edible flowers such as borage or johnny jump-ups.

Community Supported Agriculture farms, or CSAs,

CSA's offer prepaid subscriptions to the farm's produce for the season. Most CSAs offer shareholders a basket every week of the veggies and herbs that are in season on the farm. Shares vary from farm to farm, sometimes even including eggs, cheeses, flowers, and meat. Some CSAs even offer shares that go through the winter months. Becoming a member of a CSA allows you to know you're eating fresh, local food and to meet the farm and people who grow your food! You also get the satisfaction of supporting local agriculture: the prepaid CSA arrangements are a source of financial security for Vermont's farmer. CSAs have been very popular recently. Be sure to sign up early (typically in the early spring) before subscriptions are filled!

Vermont CSA Farms, are listed alphabetically by county at
www.nofavt.org

FIDDLEHEADS

When gathering wild plants, please ask for landowner permission first.

May not only brings spring weather, but fiddleheads. As mud season winds down, cars continue to crawl up and down the dirt roads, not to avoid falling into a hole, but to spot fiddleheads. Emerging from the wreckage of winter these cheerful green ferns pop up in the most unlikely places. Spotting them takes some practice, but one can always follow a slow moving car. Not all ferns are edible. Fiddlehead is a generic term, the fiddleheads that are edible belong to the ostrich fern which is a very tall elegant darn green fern when mature. They are distinctive by their dark green color and a celery-like groove on the stem. The emerging plant is what you are after and often they grow large groupings in a specific area. Pick the tightly curled fiddlehead, always leaving two or three to emerge into ferns. One wants to insure a future crop. Fiddleheads keep very well, just don't wash them until ready to cook. I have even packaged them up and mailed them to friends. They don't freeze very well though, so binge on this tasty veggie while you can. Treat fiddleheads as you would asparagus, only they are tastier. If all else fails, many Vermont super markets sell them when in season and they have even been seen at NYC markets.

Washing fiddleheads. Using two bowls, rinse the fiddleheads, pour off the water and rinse again, and again and again. Par-boil the "clean" fiddleheads for 2-3 minutes which will remove the last of the brown casing. Now you are ready to cook.

FIDDLEHEAD SOUP

1 medium bowl of cleaned fiddleheads
1 onion
1 clove of garlic
2 T butter
1 cup vegetable broth
3 cups of warm milk

In a large sauce pan, sauté the onion and garlic in the butter until tender. Add the fiddleheads to the sauce pan, reserving 10-20 nice ones, along with the broth. Cook until tender, about 10 minutes.

Puree in a food processor and return to the sauce pan. Add the warm milk and heat carefully until hot. Pour into bowls and float the reserved fiddleheads on top.

FIDDLEHEAD SALAD

½ medium bowl of cleaned fiddleheads
2-3 large red tomatoes, chopped (only hydroponic ones will be available this time of year)
½ cup feta cheese
¼ cup olive oil (sunflower oil can be used but will effect the flavor)
4 T cider vinegar

Parboil the fiddleheads to a firm consistency and then cover with cold water to stop the cooking. Drain well. Whisk together the oil and vinegar to make a dressing. Combined all of the ingredients and toss with the dressing. Best served at room temperature.

PICKLED FIDDLEHEADS

Fiddleheads can be pickled by following any basic pickling recipe or a dilly bean recipe. I have a friend who declares them the best part of his martini.

FLOUR

When George Washington was in office, King Arthur Flour started milling and selling flour and is the oldest flour company in the U.S. Although the wheat is now grown in Kansas, you get their commitment to purity; no bleach, no bromate and no chemicals of any kind. The Champlain Valley of Vermont once offered the weather and soil conditions needed for growing wheat although many other grains were grown and milled into flour. Ogden's Cider and Grist Mill, a survivor of that era, has labels for wheat, oat, rye, and barley. New Englanders traditionally preferred rye over wheat flour ('Rye' & 'Injin,') in their cornbread. Flour comes in many forms and isn't it nice to finally know what makes them different! A trip to King Arthur will offer up some very interesting varieties and, thank goodness, instructions as to their use. A good place to spend a rainy day and expand your baking knowledge.

All-purpose flour - a blended wheat flour with an intermediate gluten level, which is marketed as an acceptable compromise for most household baking needs.

Bread flour - high in gluten with a certain toughness that holds its shape well once baked. A bread machine must.

Bleached flour - treated with bleaching agents such as chlorine to whiten it (freshly milled flour is yellowish) and to give it more Gluten producing potential.

Cake flour - a finely milled flour made from soft wheat with very low gluten content, making it suitable for cakes and cookies.

Pastry flour/cookie flour/cracker flour - slightly higher in gluten content than cake flour but lower than all-purpose flour. It is suitable for fine, light-textured pastries.

Rye flour - used to bake traditional sourdough breads. Most rye breads use a mix of rye and wheat flours as rye has a low gluten content.

Pumpernickel - this bread is usually made exclusively of rye, and contains a mixture of rye flour and rye meal.

Self-rising flour - sold premixed with chemical leavening agents.

Wholewheat flour is made from the entire grain, including bran, endosperm, and germ.

POPOVERS

Without question, popovers are WOW! Making popovers is more a technique than a recipe. Having struggled through the process, and the humiliation of serving "flop overs", I thought I had it mastered. Then a friend served up fantastic popovers with a completely opposite method. So much for technique! Whatever, the results are sure to impress your family or guests. Unlike restaurant popover that hang around until served, these are best taken from the oven to the table. If you master nothing else in cooking, these will mark you as a great cook.

HOT METHOD
   1 cup flour
   2 eggs
   1 cup milk
   1 T. melted butter
   Pop over pan

Preheat the oven to 450. Butter the pan and then warm it in the oven. Take the chill off the eggs in warm water and warm the milk on the stove or microwave. Whisk in the milk with the flour, then add eggs. Stir in the melted butter. Pour the batter in the warm pan and place in the oven for 35-40 minutes. Do not open the oven! Remove and serve immediately.
If you are using a convection oven, reduce the time to 15 minutes.

COLD METHOD - **Into bowl, break 2 eggs.**
   Add 1 Cup of milk
   1 Cup of sifted flour
   1/2 t of salt.
Mix with a spoon just until eggs are well blended. Fill six well-greased custard cups 1/4 full of mixture. Set in COLD oven and turn oven on to 450 degrees. Do no open oven for 1/2 hour. Popovers should be tall and buttery brown. Remove from oven and puncture on 4 sides of neck to let out steam. Return to oven for 10 minutes with the heat off to get crusty.

From the kitchen of Kathleen Ladd's cousin Margaret

OLD TIME WHITE BREAD

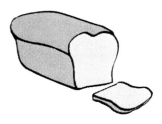

Bread is perhaps the oldest prepared foods known to man. It is basically a mixture of flour and water that is baked. It is usually leavened with yeast, microorganisms that react with moisture and heat and release carbon dioxide as part of their life cycle. The yeast is killed in the baking process but leaves a distinct flavor to the bread. The first bread maker machine was introduced in Japan in 1986. Their popularity spread and then waned once people realized how fast home-made bread went stale. No preservatives. However, that is a plus for those wanting to eat naturally, just don't leave the bread around for very long. Yeast can be purchased in bulk (much more economical than those packets) and kept in the refrigerator for 6-8 months. Local bakeries produce amazing breads well worth trying. Do keep track of the name of the maker and where it was purchased so you can return for more if it is a winner.

2 cups warm water
2/3 cup sugar
I ½ T bread starter
½ t salt
¼ cup oil
6 cups bread flour

In a large bowl, dissolve the sugar in the warm water and stir in the starter. The mixture will "proof" to a creamy white foam which means the yeast is "working." Mix the salt and oil into the mixture, adding the flour 1 cup at a time. Place in a greased bowl, cover and allow it to rise until it doubles, about an hour. Punch the dough down, knead it slightly but do

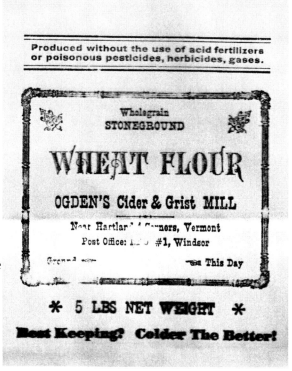

Produced without the use of acid fertilizers or poisonous pesticides, herbicides, gases.

Wholegrain
STONEGROUND

WHEAT FLOUR

OGDEN'S Cider & Grist MILL

Near Hartland Corners, Vermont
Post Office: ___ #1, Windsor

Ground ___   ___ This Day

* 5 LBS NET WEIGHT *

Best Keeping! Colder The Better!

not overwork, and divide in two. Shape each piece into loaves and place in well-oiled 9x5 loaf pans. Allow to rise in a warm place, about 30 minutes at which point the dough will rise about an inch above the pan. Bake in a preheated 350 degree oven for 40-50 minutes or until brown on top.

PANCAKES

Pancakes are just about a universal food with each country or region having their own version of this simple but delightful dish. Some countries, including Canada, have a national pancake day on Shrove Tuesday, the day before Lent

1 cup all-purpose flour
2 T sugar
2 t baking powder
1/2 t salt
1 large egg, slightly beaten
2 T sunflower oil
Milk, just enough to make the batter pour

Combine dry ingredients. Stir in egg, oil, and enough milk for batter to pour easily. Mix lightly to blend. Cook pancakes on a hot, well greased griddle. Serve with warm Vermont maple syrup!

MOTHER'S DROPPED PANCAKES

Vermont pancakes are supposed to be heavier, made from wheat or oatmeal flour but the recipe that I found for traditional Vermont pancakes is far from that. Handed down from Grandmother Sarah Atwood Fletcher to Hannah Fletcher Lear to Anna Isabel Lear Johnson to Vera Lydia Tewksbury Johnson to Emily Johnson Abbott, this is the real thing! When I asked how to make sour milk, I was met with a stare. Seems sour milk was easy to come by back then! If you don't have any, you can make your own or use sour cream.

    2 cup sour milk
    ½ t salt
    1 t baking soda
    1 egg
    Fat for deep frying (lard or oil)
Flour enough to make a stiff batter. This is measured by dipping a

teaspoon into the batter and if the spoon stands up, it's stiff! Emily likes to use bread flour. But if you want more holes use pastry flour. I suppose you could use cake flour too. Fry in deep fat as you would doughnuts. The batter will float, drop and float back to the top. That means they are done. Dip in Vermont maple syrup.
From the kitchen of Emily Johnson Abbott

To make your own sour milk, put a tablespoon of cider vinegar into a liquid measuring cup. Add milk until you have a cup of liquid. Let the mixture sit at room temperature for about 15 minutes. After this time the milk should be somewhat thick and lumpy when stirred and taste mildly sour.

PIE CRUST DOUGH

2 cups flour
2/3 cup butter, softened
2-6 T cold water

It's not the ingredients that makes good pie crust, it's technique. Cut the butter into the flour just enough to mix it. One tablespoon at a time, add the water until the dough starts to stick together. Then add one more tablespoon. Flour your hands and work the dough into two balls with a minimum of kneading. The more you work the dough, the tougher it will get. Place the dough on a floured surfaced, add more flour if it starts to stick, and roll out a circle, rolling the dough in all directions. Use a spatula to fold the dough over in half and lift into the pie plate.
From the kitchen of my mother, Eugenie Totten

FRIED PIES

4 cups flour
¾ t salt
2 t baking powder
6 T butter
2 eggs
1 cup milk
Dried applesauce
Thick cream
Granulated maple sugar

Dried applesauce

"Look over, wash thoroughly and soak fifteen minutes in clear, warm water; drain, cover with cold soft water, place on the stove, let boil slowly for two to four hours, mash fine, sweeten, and season with cinnamon very highly. Never add sugar until about five minutes before removing from the stove, otherwise the fruit will be toughened and hardened. Cook in porcelain, and do not stir while cooking."
Buckeye Cookery & Practical Housekeeping, 1877

Sift the flour, salt and baking powder together three times. Cut in the butter with a pastry fork. Beat the eggs, add the milk, and beat them into the dry mixture. Roll the dough out thing and cut it into 5 inch circles. Fry them in deep, hot fat until the cakes re golden brown. Make a heap of four fried cakes, thickly spreading warm dried applesauce between each. These are now the pies. Cut a wedge sized piece and serve it with thick cream and a bowl of granulated maple sugar. No one has ever asked for seconds!

BISCUIT DOUGH

Bisquick is a pre-mixed baking product consisting of flour, shortening, salt and baking powder. It was created by a train dining car chef in 1930 who mixed lard and the dry ingredients for biscuits ahead of time. The recipe was adapted, using hydrogenated oil, thus eliminating the need for refrigeration.

Substitution: For 1 cup Bisquick

1 cup flour,
1 1/2 t baking powder
1/2 t salt
1 t melted butter, cut in

EMPTYIN'S

Called such as so much bread was made from this that the crock was always "emptyin'."

2 T flour
½ t salt
1 T maple sugar
2 cups warmed milk

Combine all of the ingredients and mix into a smooth paste. Pour into a crockery pitcher and leave in a warm place for 3-4 days until the mixture clabbers. Use this to start bread and rolls.

GAME BIRDS

QUAIL, PHEASANT, PARTRIDGE

Thanks to the increase of farms that raise game birds for meat production it is no longer necessary to grab a gun to get your own. Specially raised and processed for consumers, quail and pheasant are quite available. However, the partridge will be a bit harder to find even though it is the most common game bird hunted in Vermont. Admittedly, the commercial quail and pheasant breeds are not native Vermont birds, but they are produced here. The product comes whole, semi-boneless, boneless (legs and wings still have bones) and butterflied.

QUAIL SALAD

4 quail, semi-boneless
2-3 pears, cored and sliced
6 bacon strips, chopped
1 bunch green onions or 4-5 ramps, chopped
3 T cider jelly
¼ cup cider vinegar
2-3 T butter
4 oz mixed greens or arugula
Salt and pepper

Season both sides of the quail with salt and pepper. In a large sauté pan add 2-3 T of butter and bring up to medium heat. Sauté the quail, breast side down, for 4-5 minutes on each side. Remove from the pan and reserve. Using the same pan, add bacon and cook until lightly browned, add pears and green onions or ramps and cook for 2-3 minutes. If using ramps, be careful not to overcook. Add the cider jelly and vinegar to the mix, cook until pears are just soft and there is still liquid in the pan. Turn off heat. Toss the pear mixture over greens and place the quail on top and serve

RASPBERRY PHEASANT

2 pheasant, boneless breasts
½ cup water
¼ cup maple syrup
1 cup raspberries (fresh or frozen)
2 T balsamic vinegar
½ t salt
½ t black pepper

Bring ½ cup water to a boil in a small saucepan and dissolve the
maple syrup in it. Add raspberries and boil gently for five minutes.
Press through a sieve to remove seeds, then stir in vinegar, salt and
pepper. Marinate pheasant breasts in raspberry sauce, refrigerated
for a least two hours and as long as overnight. Drain pheasant,
reserving marinade, and sauté in 2 T oil over medium heat for 7
minutes on each side or until no longer pink inside. Add marinade
and turn meat several times to coat well with hot sauce and serve.

HUNTER'S PARTRIDGE

4 partridges
4 cups cabbage, shredded
4 slices bacon, cooked and crumbles
16 large cabbage leaves
2 T butter
1 cup chicken or vegetable broth
4 carrots, sliced
¼ t crushed thyme
1.4 t tarragon
Salt and pepper

Sprinkle partridges inside and out with salt and pepper. Combine
shredded cabbage and bacon and spoon a fourth of the mixture
inside the cavity of each of the four birds. Wrap each bird with 4
cabbage leaves and fasten with a string. Place in a large skillet, add
butter, broth, and remaining ingredients. Bring liquid to boil, reduce
heat, cover, and simmer 25 to 30 minutes or until tender. Remove
string and cabbage leaves. Serve with sauce in pan.

GOAT (CHEVON)

The New York Times front page had a picture of a goat just before Easter to educate its readers that goat, although not in America, is the most widely consumed meat in the world. Lower in fat than chicken and higher in protein than beef, its taste was described as, "Think lamb, but with a tang of earthy darkness." There are a lot of goat farms in Vermont, some dairies and some raising them for meat. I have a pet goat, Nudge, and really balked about including this for his sake. However, since a doe produces twins every year, it is obvious that those boy goats don't all get to be pets. Goat meat is lean, best braised or cooked with moist heat.

GOAT RAGU

3/4 cup olive oil or substitute
1 1/2 pounds ground goat meat
1/2 cup finely diced carrot
1/2 cup finely diced onion
1/2 cup finely diced celery
1 T tomato paste
1 1/2 cups red wine
1 cup diced tomatoes
3 cups chicken broth or water
2 bay leaves
1/4 t chile pepper seeds or flakes
1/2 t ground cumin
1/2 t ground coriander
1/2 t ground fennel
1 T fresh thyme leaves
1 T fresh rosemary leaves
1/2 t salt
1/4 t ground pepper

Place a large stewpot or skillet over medium-high heat. Heat oil and add goat meat, stirring to break it up. Raise heat to high and cook until browned, about 5 minutes. Spoon off excess liquid. Add carrot, onion and celery, stirring for about 2 minutes. Add tomato paste and stir until blended, about 1 minute. Add wine and stir, scraping bottom of pan, until completely evaporated, about 2 minutes; adjust

51

heat as necessary to prevent burning. Add tomatoes, chicken broth or water, bay leaves, chile pepper flakes, cumin, coriander, fennel, thyme, rosemary, salt and pepper. Bring to a boil, then reduce heat to medium-low. Simmer uncovered until most of the liquid evaporates, about 1 1/2 hours, scraping down sides of pot as necessary to avoid burning. Meat will turn dark brown and liquid dark orange.

APPLE BRAISED CHEVON CHOPS

4-6 chevon (goat) chops
½ -1 cup apple cider
½ cup currants
2 T butter
Salt and pepper

Brown chops on each side in a frying pan with 2 T. butter. Pour enough cider to cover the bottom of the frying pan with ¼ inch of juice. Cover pan and simmer about 15 minutes, then turn, adding apple slices and currants. Cook another 15 minutes. Timing may vary depending on the size of the chops. Strain and serve with cooked fruit.

Vermont Fresh Network

Dedicated to connecting farmers, food producers and chefs to support Vermont agriculture and bring fresh, flavorful, high-quality food to all Vermonters.

A strong farm economy creates local jobs, provides nutritious food and preserves the close-knit communities of Vermont. The Vermont Fresh Network helps farms and restaurants team up to provide the freshest local food at restaurants.

Annual forum – Shelburne Farms

The Vermont Fresh Network PO Box 895,
Richmond, VT 05477
802.434.2000
info@vermontfresh.net

GREEN BEANS

Green beans are the unripe fruit of any bean, hence the term "green." Harvest timing determines the quality of the vegetable, left too long on the vine and the beans will have starched up and become tough to eat. Green beans come in colors other than green; yellow (wax), purple (turn green when cooked), red or streaked. Also known as snap beans, string beans, wax beans or hericot vert (French). Green beans come in two major groups, bush and pole. If you plan on growing your own, read the seed packet carefully in order to properly prepare a place for the plant to grow. Pole beans, just like Jack and the Beanstalk, will grow up and up and up. Shapes range; long, thin, short and wide. With 130 varieties to choose from it is fun to grow more than one kind. The beauty of green beans is that they freeze very well. The best method I have used is to just cover the fresh beans with water and bring to a boil. Remove and pour the beans, water and all, in a freezer bag and freeze immediately. Thaw the entire bag and heat in the water frozen in. The beans are crispy and taste great. Refreeze the water and use as vegetable broth when making soups as it is full of vitamins and flavor.

EAT 'EM RAW

There is nothing like the taste and crunch of a freshly picked green bean. Half of mine never make it out of the garden! Having more than one color bean makes for a festive dish. Wash, drain and serve with the dip of your choice. Slice lengthwise and put them in a salad. Or just eat them plain.

Spiced up Mayonnaise – Combine mayonnaise with hot pepper juice or bits to taste. Dip into with the peas and enjoy.

Ramp Dip – Dice 2-4 ramps, depending on taste (ramp flavor will develop with storage, be careful), and mix with sour cream or plain yogurt.

Fiddlehead Mole – Mole means concoction. Starting with cooked fiddleheads (finely chopped or pureed), develop your own mole by adding tomatoes, chile tomatoes, onion, garlic, sugar, bread crumbs, cilantro, currants, etc. The more ingredients, the better the mole.

DILLY BEANS – A VERMONT TRADITION

Since green beans produce right up to frost there has always been the question of how to preserve the ones not eaten. A long time Vermont tradition was to pickle them with dill, hence the name. There are many variations of the recipe, this being just one. If you don't like it, there are plenty more to try from many different sources.

3 lbs green beans
1 ½ t cayenne pepper – ¼ t in each pint
6 peeled garlic cloves – 1 in each pint
6 dill heads – 1 in each pint
12 T dill seed – 2 T in each pint
3 ¼ cups vinegar
3 ½ cups water
6 T salt

Pack the beans in jars leaving some head room. Add spices to each pint. Boil the water, vinegar and salt and fill each jar. Process according to your canners instructions. Allow to stand for twelve days before opening. This recipe also works with fiddleheads.

STRING BEANS WITH VERMONT SMOKED HAM

Salty meats, such as bacon and ham, have long been companions of string beans, especially in the south. This is the Vermont version.

1/4 pound string beans (fresh or frozen)
2 T butter
3 ounces Vermont smoked ham, finely chopped
1 minced shallot
3 T minced parsley (fresh or frozen)
2 cloves minced garlic

Cook or reheat beans depending on whether they are fresh or frozen. Drain and set aside. Melt the butter in a skillet over medium heat and sauté the ham, garlic and shallot until brown, about 2 minutes. Add the beans and parsley and sauté until hot. Serve immediately.

HERBS & SEASONING

Trotting out to the herb garden to garner fresh plants while cooking is a luxury. Next best is drying, freezing or preserving herbs for use all year. Following instructions on drying herbs, hang plants in late summer and fall from a rack in the kitchen and enjoy filling the house with wonderful aromas.

Herbs that dry well;
**Basil - Oregano - Sage - Thyme - Rosemary -
Mint - Chamomile - Rose hips - Lemon Balm**

Herbs should be thoroughly dry before placing in an airtight container for long term storage.

Garlic and Garlic scapes
When the garlic forms tops, scapes, in the late Spring, snip them off and steam them whole and serve with melted butter or cut them into short lengths to add to soups or grilled cheese sandwiches. They have a delicate garlic taste. They also make a great pesto that can be frozen. Harvest and air dry the garlic cloves for use all year.

Chile peppers
The hotness of chile peppers is concentrated on the interior ribs, if they have a yellow/orange color, it will be a hot one. They can be dried in the sun, on the shelf above the back seat of a car, in an oven, or string them up and air dry.

Herbs that freeze well;

Parsley - Chives - Basil
Cut the parsley and arrange on a cookie sheet but don't overcrowd. Place the cookie sheet freezer, uncovered, for 20 minutes. Working fast, so that the leaves don't thaw, brush into a freezer bag and place back in the freezer. The parsley will keep all winter with a nice green color. Use directly from the bag.

Chives do not freeze well with this method, nor do they dry well. But they do freeze well in water. Use an ice cube tray and fill each space 1/3 full with freshly snipped chives. Cover with water and freeze. Remove the cubes and place in a freezer bag. The cubes can be dropped directly into soup or thawed and drained. The chives might need a bit of squeezing to rid them of extra water. Excellent in egg salad.

Basil also freezes well in water in ice cube trays.

JAPANESE KNOTWEED

Listed by the World Conservation Union as one of the world's 100 worst invasive species, it came from Japan to Vermont as a decorative garden plant. It now chokes waterways, crowds out native species and is extremely difficult to eradicate. But, if you can beat 'em, eat 'em. When young, Japanese Knotweed has a Granny Smith apple/rhubarb taste. The shoots need to be cut early when they are 12-18 inches high, mid-April through May. Doubtful that anyone would complain about cutting knotweed, but do ask for landowner permission first. The shoots are hollow so pick thick ones so they will yield more when peeled. Scrape off the thin, red, outer skin with a knife or peeler and chop the shoots into 1"-2" pieces. They can be used for any recipe calling for rhubarb or eaten raw.

KNOTWEED CAKE

4 cups firmly packed Japanese knotweed pieces
3 eggs
1 ¼ cups sugar
2 t apple brandy
¼ t salt
2 cups flour
1 t baking soda
2 t cinnamon
¼ t allspice
¼ t nutmeg
1 cup applesauce

Preheat oven to 350 degrees. Grease a 13" by 9" baking pan. Beat eggs, sugar, salt and apple brandy in a large mixing bowl until blended. Mix the flour, baking soda and spices together in a separate bowl. Add the flour mixture to the egg mixture, then add the applesauce, knotweed pieces and mix until blended. Pour the batter into the greased baking pan and spread evenly. Bake for one hour, then remove from the oven and cool on a wire drying rack. .

KNOTWEED AND DIP

Prepare the knotweed stalks as described above and cut into bite size pieces. Store wrapped tightly in cellophane until using as they will dry out. Serve with dip of choice.

JELLY AND JAM

The only difference between jelly and jam is that jelly is strained to remove the seeds. There are some fruits that you definitely do not want to include the seeds, such as rose hips. Jellies can be made from a wide variety of fruits, leaves, roots, or blossoms and is sometimes the only option of what to do with a bumper crop. Depending on the pectin product you choose to use, follow the directions on the box as there are slight differences between products. Or, you can extract your own pectin from green apples.

The first step is to prepare a plant extract and that can be kept refrigerated or frozen until you are ready to use it.

FROM BLOSSOMS (violet, dandelion, clover, rose, etc.) or **LEAVES** (mint, thyme, etc.) - Pick out any dead or dried blossoms. Pour 1 quart boiling water over 1-4 cups blossoms. Use smaller quantity for strongly flavored flowers like dandelion and greater quantity for delicate flowers like violet. Set in refrigerator overnight. Strain and proceed with jelly-making. Violet jelly has a lovely color and unique taste.

FROM ROOTS (sassafras, ginger, etc.) - simmer in water, strain, add water if too strongly flavored. Proceed with jelly-making.

FROM FRUITS, BERRIES (rose hips, berries, grapes, pears, apricots, plums, etc.) - simmer in a little water, strain, proceed with jelly-making.

FROM LIQUIDS (apple cider, hard apple cider, grape juice) Proceed directly with jelly-making.

LAMB

The introduction of Merino sheep to Vermont caused a boon that resulted in over 1 million sheep by 1837, that was 5 ½ sheep per person. Raised primarily for wool, lambs were a sheep by-product put on the table. Today, a visit to the Vermont Sheep and Goat Festival in Tunbridge, Vermont, will give you an idea of the variety of sheep raised in the state. Grass-fed herds of Shetland, Basque, Katahdin, Jacob and other interesting heirloom breeds produce wool, cheese and meat for a growing sheep industry in Vermont. Lambs can be ordered ahead to insure availability.

HERBED LAMB

Lamb shoulder or lamb shanks, ½ to ¾ pound per person
Fresh or dried herbs of choice, rosemary, dill, oregano, basil
Butter
Vegetable broth, water or white or red wine

The night before, prepare a wet rub from melted butter mixed with the herb of your choice or a combination. A wet rub will help keep the meat from drying out and should have the consistency of a thick paste. Do not over season. Two hours before serving, cover the bottom of a skillet with enough butter to brown the lamb pieces, about 15 minutes. Remove to a covered ovenproof pan and add enough liquid (water, broth, red or white wine) to fill the pan about ½ inch deep. Bake at 325 degrees for two hours, checking from time to time to add liquid should it get low.

MAPLE GLAZED LAMB CHOPS

6 Lamb chops
1 shallot
1 clove garlic
1 T rosemary or herb of choice
1 T mustard
2 cups beef stock
1 T red wine
2 T butter
Salt and pepper
Mashed potatoes or cooked greens

Combine the beef stock and wine in a sauce pan, uncovered, and bring to a boil, simmering, until it is reduced to ½ cup, about an hour. This step can be done ahead. The liquid should be thick and coat a spoon. Season lamb chops evenly with salt and pepper. In a medium sauté pan melt the butter as hot as you can without burning and sear the lamb chops, 1 minute on each side. Remove and keep warm. Pour off all excess fat from the pan and return it to the heat. Add 1 T butter, shallots and garlic and sauté for 30 seconds. Add the maple syrup, mustard, reduced beef stock and herbs to the pan and stir together, cooking the mixture until it thickens to a sauce consistency. Add the lamb chops back into the pan, cooking for an additional 30 seconds (for medium rare), basting the chop to cover with a glaze. Serve in a hot plate over mashed potatoes or slightly cooked greens and drizzle with remaining sauce.

BONELESS LEG OF LAMB WITH GARLIC

1 boneless leg of lamb (4 to 4 1/2 pounds)
8 large heads of garlic plus 2 cloves
Oil
2 t fresh or dried rosmary
1 t fresh or dried thyme

Place the oven rack in the lower third of the oven and preheat to 425 degrees. Place the lamb roast, cut side down, in an oiled roasting pan just large enough to fit. Cut the 2 cloves of garlic into slivers and, making cuts in the lamb, insert a garlic sliver. Coat with oil and herbs. Roast for 15 minutes, then reduce the heat to 350 degrees. Roast until an internal thermometer reads 125 degrees, about 1 1/2 hours. About 40 minutes before the lamb is due to be done, place the 8 cloves of garlic in the oven wrapped in foil. Remove the lamb and allow to stand for 15 minutes before carving. Slice the lamb across the grain. Skim the fat from the surface and spoon the juices over the lamb. Unwrap the garlic and serve along side.
From the kitchen of Renee Novello

Consider lamb with ramp pesto or rosehip jelly on the side

MAPLE SYRUP

The origin of maple syrup goes back to Native Americans, they, in turn, give credit to the squirrels. A small tooth mark in the bark of a sugar maple tree produced a sweet drip of sap which the squirrels lapped up. The Native Americans quickly devised ways to collect the liquid and found that by removing the top layer of ice each morning that the remaining liquid became yellow and sweeter. The final step was to boil it down over a fire. In the 1800's, many Vermont farms earned their tax money by making syrup with up to 1,000 maple trees in their "sugar bush". I encourage everyone to take the time to watch the process. Not hard, as come late February and into March the air is thick with aroma coming from sugarhouses boiling sap day and night. It is not until one makes one's own syrup, however, that one can appreciate the effort required, and therefore the price, of the product. I will refer you to "Backyard Sugarin'" by Rink Mann as an excellent guide through the process. There are so many things one can do with maple syrup other than pouring on pancakes, be inventive.

Rule of thumb when substituting with maple syrup
¾ cup maple syrup = 1 cup of sugar

Mix the syrup with the liquid in the recipe, not the dry ingredients. If the recipe calls for butter or shortening, melt it and mix with the maple syrup. You may add ¼ to ½ t baking soda to neutralize the syrup's slight acidity unless the recipe uses yogurt, buttermilk or sour cream. Decrease the cooking temperature by 25 degrees.

SUGAR ON SNOW

No one should die without having this experience. Perhaps the best sugar high you will ever experience, it is advised not to take your kids to church right after indulging. Sugar on snow is traditionally served with sour pickles to cut the sweetness of the candy. Having read that, how can you resist?

1 quart of pure maple syrup
1 cup (2 sticks) butter
1 tub of packed snow (chipped ice works too)
Candy thermometer

Heat the syrup and butter in a large pot over medium heat, watch carefully as you do not want it to boil over.

Using the candy thermometer, bring the syrup to 234 degrees F and then immediately test by spooning a tablespoon of the syrup over the snow. If the syrup takes on a taffy consistency, it is ready. Pour "ribbons" over the snow and eat in bowls.

VERMONT FRENCH TOAST

Thickly sliced bread
2 eggs
2/3 cup milk
½ cup pure maple syrup
2 T cream
Butter

Beat the eggs until light, whisk in the milk, maple syrup and cream. Soak the bread slices, one at a time, in the mixture. Heat a large skillet or griddle over medium heat, buttered lightly. Cook the bread 2-3 minutes per side or until golden brown. Serve with warm maple syrup.

MAPLE CUSTARD

3 eggs
½ cup maple syrup
2 cups milk
Dash of salt

Preheat the oven to 350 degrees. Mix the ingredients and pour into individual custard cups or ramekins. Set the cups in a pan of water that reaches at least ½ way up the cups. Bake for about 40 minutes or until a knife comes out clean when inserted in the custard. Serve warm, perhaps with warm maple syrup drizzled over the top.

SMOKED MAPLE SYRUP

Truly original, this Vermont made product offers a unique flavor for cooking. Using a cold smoke process, the syrup is smoked with select apple and maple wood for over a week giving the end product a delicate, smooth and mellow flavor with no bitter aftertaste. Smoked syrup is best applied at the end of the cooking process. Cooking it too long will dissipate the delicate "smokiness." Since this product is made only during cool weather it is not always available which makes it even more alluring. Be creative!

Also see:
Pork Chop and Apple with Smoked Maple Syrup
Artisan Grilled Cheese Sandwich
Pears on Toast with Melted Brie and Smoked Maple Syrup

MILK & GOAT MILK

Our ancestors would be amazed to learn that we buy all of the products that they daily made from milk at home. Pasteurization is partially responsible and, although an important heath benefit, it removed the bacteria that, allowed the right temperature and time, produced many different dairy products. Some we still know, some have been lost over time and some have become gourmet items. Many are now Vermont-made at both large and small dairies with demonstrations and recipes available to visitors. There are many recipes on how to make any of these products at home, the benefit being freshness and lack of preservatives. Some store bought products, such as buttermilk and yogurt, still contain active bacteria cultures that can be employed to make more of the same or diversify into some fun milk products. If you need raw milk, i.e. unpasteurized, there is a growing number of dairies offering that product. Goat milk is also quite easy to find and is the answer for those lactose intolerant. Raw milk has become increasingly popular for children as it still contains some of the vitamins and enzymes that make digestion easier. Only certified dairies can sell raw milk and only directly to the customer at the farm. Raw milk cheese is also becoming more popular.

Sweet milk – fresh milk.

Sour milk – milk we would throw away but our great grandmothers used for all sorts of things. Sour milk can be made by adding a tablespoon of apple cider vinegar and letting the milk sit at room temperature for 15 minutes. *See Emily's drop pancakes.*

Butter and "old fashioned" Buttermilk - Farm families would let fresh milk sit for half a day skimming off the cream which had risen. Naturally occurring bacteria would cause it to slightly sour which increased the efficiency of churning for butter. When the butter was removed, the remaining liquid was called buttermilk.

Cultured buttermilk – What we are familiar with today. It can be made by adding a bacteria starter to fresh milk and letting it "clabber" for a day, or so.

Evaporated milk – Created in the late 1800's as a way to keep milk without refrigeration, it is basically milk that has been reduced by 60% and sterilized. The high heat from sterilization gives it a caramelized flavor. There is even evaporated goat milk!

Clabbered cream – Unpasteurized milk, allowed to set, will separate the cream to the top. Allowed to sit for several days, bacteria in the milk will cause the top of the cream to thicken and slightly sour. Clabbered cream will react with baking soda and produce a leavening reaction for baking (Clabber Girl baking soda). It can also be used to make sour cream & cottage cheese. *See Emptyin's*

Loppered milk – Another term for clabbered milk but a bit more specific as it refers to the layer just below the butter cream and was used to make cottage cheese. In that process, if heated too long, an extremely tough substance was the result. In 1897, an enterprising gentleman developed a process to make buttons from loppered milk.

Cottage cheese – Curdled milk. The curds are the cheese.

Farmer cheese – Pressed cottage cheese which removes most of the moisture.

Sour cream – Dating back centuries, sour cream was made by letting fresh cream sour naturally. Bacteria in the cream, including Streptococcus and Lactobacillus, created the acid flavor in the cream. Today's product is pasteurized to prevent it from becoming too sour.

Crème Fraiche – Originated in France, it is made in a similar fashion to sour cream but without adding bacteria. The process requires a number of careful steps to maintain high viscosity although the original farm product was simply the result of milk sitting out. It is now a gourmet item. A fair facsimile can be made at home.

Devon cream – An English clotted cream used for desserts. It is the semi-solid layer of cream that forms when unpasteurized milk is heated. Now a gourmet item.

Yogurt – Another century old milk product, it is made by allowing Lactobacillus bacteria to ferment the lactose in the milk to produce an acidic (helps preserve) and easily digestible product.

Cream cheese - An American invention developed in 1872, it pairs cream with a mesophilic starter culture and rennet to produce a creamy, spreadable cheese.

Ice cream – Until 1851, ice cream was only made at home and known as cream ice. The hand cranked churns were replaced by two stroke engines and ice cream making demonstrations can be seen at many Vermont country fairs.

PEACHES, APRICOTS AND PLUMS

In Vermont? "The History of Vermont, Natural, Civil and Statistical," published in 1842 states, "That as good peaches may be raised in Vermont as in any other place, we think will hardly be disputed by any who ate of those which grew in our own garden in Burlington during the past and present year. In the northern parts of the state, the native, or Canada Plum is much cultivated. It bears plentifully, and the fruit is tolerable. Our plum trees generally are very uncertain bearers. After bearing profusely one year, they often pass several years without producing any fruit." Southern Vermont College, in Bennington, Vermont, once had 3,000 plum trees as part of its orchard. Plum trees can still be found in the remnants of old orchards but are rarely recognized for what they are until they produce fruit. 95% of the apricots, origin China, grown in the United States come from California. Less than ¼ of the crop goes to market fresh as they do not travel well. Therefore, finding fresh apricots in Vermont might not be easy, but it is possible. Although winter hardy, a spring frost is a limiting factor when it comes to bearing fruit. A friend, living near Lake Champlain, planted an apricot tree and four years later harvested 500 pounds of apricots! That is a lot of jam. The peach, also from China, can also thrive in Vermont although temperatures below minus 15 degrees will kill off the buds resulting in no crop. The plum is the hardiest of the three. Orchards in the Champlain Valley are the best bet to find these delicious fruits.

PEACH SOUP

The beauty of this dish is that it can be made from fresh or canned peaches.

> **1 pound of fresh or canned peaches, unsweetened.**
> **1 T honey**
> **1 T fresh or 1 t dried rosemary**
> **1 T or less hard apple cider**
> **2 T sugar**
> **4 T sour cream or plain yogurt**
> **3 T applejack or Vermont fruit brandy**

If fresh, peel the peaches and cook until soft in just enough water to cover them. If canned, cook until hot. In both cases, cook with the

64

rosemary. While still hot, puree. Mix in the honey, taste and adjust the sweetness with the hard apple cider, it won't take much. Mix the sugar with the yogurt and, after ladling the soup into a small bowl, dollop on top. Drizzle the applejack or brandy on top. Serve hot.

APRICOT CHICKEN SALAD

4 cups of cooked chicken, diced.
1 stalk of celery, finely diced.
2 T onion, finely chopped.
3 large sweet apricots, pitted and finely diced.
Mayonnaise.
Salt and pepper.

Combine all ingredients, mayonnaise last. Season to taste. Serve as a salad or make a great sandwich.

PLUM CLAFOUTI

A clafouti is a custard-like baked dish made with fresh fruit. French in origin, it is a lovely way to showcase fresh fruit in a dessert. This is also a great dish with pears or fresh berries.

¼ cup of sugar plus 1 T of sugar
¾ lb plums halved, pitted
¾ cup of milk
¾ cup of light cream
¾ cup of flour
2 eggs
1 egg yolk
Pinch of salt

Preheat the oven to 400 degrees and butter a pie plate well. Sprinkle the pie plate with 1 T of the sugar and arrange the plum halves, skin side down, in the plate. In a blender or food processor, combine the milk, light cream, flour, eggs, egg yolk and salt for 2 minutes. Add the ¼ cup of sugar and blend for a few more seconds. Pour the mixture over the plums and bake in the middle of the oven for 30 minutes or until puffed and golden. The fruit will rise to the top and offer a beautiful plum color. Serve hot.

PEARS

Tucked into many Vermont apple orchards is a pear tree or two. Often overlooked as barren apple trees, a closer look will reveal lovely green pears of amazing sweetness and taste. Pears are sneaky as they don't produce every year and when they do, can ripen practically overnight and drop the whole crop for the benefit of wandering wildlife. In other words, if you see a pear, pick it.

FRESH PEAR TART

1 unbaked pie shell (*see Pie Crust Dough*)
Custard
    6 T white flour
    ¾ cup butter
    2/3 cup sugar
    3 eggs
    1 t vanilla extract
    1/4 t grated nutmeg
    Enough fruit to line the bottom of the pie dish

Sift the flour and nutmeg. Met the butter. Remove from the heat and add the sugar. Whisk in the four nutmeg mixture. Stir in the eggs, one at a time, then the vanilla. At this point the custard should be thick and smooth. Arrange the fruit in the pie shell, cover with the custard. Bake at 350 for 45-50 minutes until the custard is firm and golden.

PEAR UPSIDE DOWN SPICE CAKE

Both spice cakes and upside-down cakes are part of New England's culinary heritage which might be news to most people. New England sailing vessels often brought back pineapples and spices from their Caribbean voyages. Pineapples were popular even in colonial times and became the symbol of hospitality due to the serving of pineapple upside down cakes to guests. But the recipe started with pears and quite frankly, should have remained so. This dessert is outstanding.

6 -10 pears (enough to cover the bottom of your pan)
6 T butter
1/3 cup sugar
1/2 cup light brown sugar

Cake
    6 T butter
    3 T packed light brown sugar
    2 eggs separated (2 of the whites included in the next
    ingredient)
    4 egg whites
    1/2 cup molasses
    1 cup sifted cake flour
    1 t baking soda
    1/2 t salt
    1 t ground ginger
    1 t ground cinnamon
    1 t ground nutmeg
(There are a lot of non-local ingredients here, but being a historical
recipe, forgive)

The historical recipe calls for an ovenproof skillet to bake the cake in.
You can also use a more modern cake pan with a removable bottom.
However, if you choose the later, place the cake pan on a cookie sheet
when preparing and baking as some of the liquid will leak.

Peel and core the pear, cut into 1/2 inch slices. Toss the pears in a
hot saute pan with 2 T butter and the sugar until the pears are nicely
browned and the sugar is caramelized. You might need to add 2 T
water but don't if the pears are juicy. Remove from the heat, set aside.
Combine the 1/2 cup brown sugar and 4 T butter in a nonstick
skillet and cook gently over low heat until a syrup forms. Arrange
the pears in a circular pattern over the syrup (caution, very hot)-
OR- arrange the pears on the bottom of a cake pan and pour the
syrup over it. Do this carefully and artistically as the pears will
be on top. Preheat the oven to 350. To make the spice cake batter,
cream butter with brown sugar in a mixing bowl, beating until light
and fluffy. Beat in the egg yolks from the separated eggs. Stir in
the molasses. Sift the flour, baking soda, salt, and spices. Fold into
the batter, do not over mix. Beat the egg whites until stiff peaks
form. Fold into the batter a third at a time. Spread the batter evenly

over the pears in the skillet or cake pan. Bake for about 35 minutes or until the center of the cake springs back when touched. To unmold, place a serving plate over the pan and turn it, inverting the cake onto the plate. Serve warm or at room temperature.

PEAR COMPOTE

Common preparation of a compote is a cooked dish of fresh or dried fruit simmered whole or in pieces in a sugar syrup. Traditional Vermont compotes called for dried fruit and that substitute can be made in this recipe, just add water to cook. Drying can be as easy as cutting up the fruit and placing it on screens in a cool, dry place in the house. Variations of this recipe can be cooking and serving whole or halved fruit. Compotes can be served as breakfast, as their own dessert or as a base for other desserts such as fruit tarts where fresh fruit is layered over the compote which is held in a baked pastry shell. Get creative!

6-10 pears
½ cup maple syrup
½ cup heavy cream

Peel, core and seed the pears. Place in a cooking pot and pour in the maple syrup. Bring to a boil, then simmer carefully for 15-20 minutes or until the pears are soft. Remove the pears and cook the liquid another 15-20 minutes until reduced to a syrup. Add the pears and puree. Chill. Before serving, whip the heavy cream and fold into the pear puree. Garnish with fresh pears and mint.

AUTUMN PEAR SALAD

Late greens, made a wonderful compliment to pears. The spicy taste of arugula and the color of the beet green stems really makes this salad. You can plant as late as September to get a bonus crop of fresh greens, most of which will survive a light frost.

Assortment of greens including arugula and beet greens
5 pears
1/2 cup Feta cheese

Wash and toss the greens. Slice the pears, removing the core and seeds (peeling the skin is optional). Toss in just enough Feta cheese to sprinkle the salad white. Serve at room temperature.

PEARS ON TOAST WITH MELTED BRIE

Ripe pears, sliced to 1/3 inch with core removed. Skin on.
Brie cheese
Toasted bread of choice
Smoked maple syrup

Use your favorite crusty bread to make rounds or toast points (triangles). On each piece of toast place a 1/3 inch slice of ripe pear and top it with a piece of Brie cheese. Bake in a 350 degree oven until the Brie melts. Remove from oven and drizzle with Smoked Maple Syrup. Serve as an hors d'oeuvre or as a unique dessert.

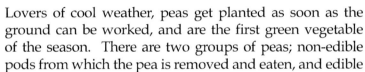

PEAS

Lovers of cool weather, peas get planted as soon as the ground can be worked, and are the first green vegetable of the season. There are two groups of peas; non-edible pods from which the pea is removed and eaten, and edible pods where you eat everything. Of this group, snap or sugarsnap peas have a round pod whereas snow peas have a flat pod. Although there are many cooked pea dishes, they are one vegetable, in my opinion, that cannot be improved on with other ingredients. If freezing, cook the peas in just enough water to cover them and immediately freeze in that water. When thawed, reheat in the same water to retain the nutrients and flavor of the vegetable.

EAT 'EM RAW WITH DIP

There is nothing like the taste and crunch of freshly picked snap peas. Half of mine never make it out of the garden, the other half are eaten raw. Wash, drain and serve with the dip of your choice.

Spiced up Mayonnaise – Combine mayonnaise with hot pepper juice or bits to taste. Dip into with the peas and enjoy.

Ramp Dip – Dice 2-4 ramps, depending on taste (flavor will develop with storage, be careful), and mix with sour cream or plain yogurt

Fiddlehead Mole – Mole means concoction. Starting with cooked fiddleheads (finely chopped or pureed), develop your own mole by adding tomatoes, chile tomatoes, onion, garlic, sugar, bread crumbs, cilantro, currants, etc. The more ingredients in a mole, the better.

BUTTERED PEAS WITH MINT - OR NOT

3 cups of shelled peas
3 T butter
5 mint leaves, chopped (optional)
Salt and pepper

Rinse the peas and add to boiling water, cooking to your choice of texture, 2 minutes for al dente, 10 minutes for cooked. Drain, toss in a serving bowl with butter, season to taste. There is great discussion over whether the mint improves or overrides the flavor of the peas and I suggest you try both ways and decide for yourself.

PORK

"The Small Yorkshire, as a grazing pig, will do extremely as seen by fat pigs in summer which were entirely grass-fed," from Types and Breeds of Farm Animals, 1905. Pastured pigs are obviously nothing new, but hard to find until recently. A variety of grass-fed pig farms in Vermont offer products either from their farm or at local markets. What is half a pig? About 23 pork chops, 2 roasts, 1 fresh ham, 8 lbs of fresh bacon slab, 3 lbs of spare ribs, 9 lbs of ground pork, totaling about 75 lbs in the freezer. You may want to consider buying just what you need!

PORK CHOP & APPLE WITH SMOKED MAPLE SYRUP

6 pork chops
1 T butter
salt and pepper to taste
3 tart apples
3 T smoked maple syrup *(Or Molasses or maple syrup)*
3 T flour
2 cups hot water
1 T cider vinegar
1/2 cup dried cranberries+

Season the pork chops with salt and pepper. Heat the butter in a large heavy skillet and brown the pork chops on both sides. Transfer pork chops to a large shallow baking dish. Peel, core and slice apples into rings and arrange over pork chops. Drizzle the smoked maple syrup or the molasses over the pork chops and apples. To the drippings in the skillet, add flour; cook, stirring, until browned. Slowly stir in the hot water and cook until bubbly. Add vinegar and dried cranberries. Pour sauce over apples and pork chops in the baking dish. Cover and bake at 350° for 1 hour.
+Cranberries are grown in Vermont!

VERMONT PORK CHOPS

6 pork chops
¼ cup chopped onion
1 T apple cider vinegar
½ t chile pepper
1/8 t pepper
¼ cup maple syrup
¼ cup water

1 ½ t salt
Flour to thicken gravy
1-2 T butter

Preheat oven to 400 degrees. Lightly brown the outside of the chops in the butter. Combine the rest of the ingredients over low heat in a saucepan. In a flat baking dish place the pork chops and pour the sauce over the chops. Cover and cook for 45 minutes, basting occasionally. Bake uncovered for the last 15 minutes. Remove to a warm platter and thicken the sauce slightly with the flour. Pour over the pork chops and serve.

PORK WITH APPLES AND CREAM

This dish is perfect showcasing some of the best ingredients Vermont has to offer; grass fed pork, crème Fraiche, local cooking apples, hard cider and Vermont's own apple brandy.

3-4 large apples of a tart variety
1 T sugar
2 tenderloins of pork, sliced thickly on the diagonal into 6 pieces
1 large chopped onion
4-6 T butter
5 T Vermont apple brandy or applejack
1 T flour
2/3 bottle hard apple cider
2/3 cup crème Fraiche
salt and pepper to taste

Peel and slice the apples into thick pieces, sauté in butter over medium low heat until slightly soft. Sprinkle on sugar, raising the heat to caramelize. Set aside. Salt and pepper the chops. Using 2 sauté pans, melt 2 T butter in each and divide the onion, cooking until translucent. Add the meat, browning on both sides. Drain excess fat, keeping back the onions. Return the meat to the pans reheating gently and pour on all but 1 T of brandy or applejack. Warm the ladle and then light the liquid, pouring over the meat to flame. Stir until the flame dies down. Sprinkle flour over each pan, sautéing a few minutes, de-glazeing with the hard cider and stock. Cover and simmer, turning the pieces of meat over occasionally until the juices run clear. Remove pork to a warmed serving dish. Gently re-heat the sautéed apple. Combine the sauce and further reduce in one pan, lower heat and add the crème Fraiche. Arrange the apples around the pork, then pour the sauce over all.

POTATOES

While it is easy to connect potatoes with the Irish, they actually got their domestic start with the Incas. The blue potato, which has recently appeared in markets, is an heirloom from Peru. Introduced to Europe in 1588, the potato soon distinguished itself as being able to produce more food on less land than any other crop. Yet the potato had great difficulty gaining popularity until it became the hero of starving Ireland. But in 1845, the lack of crop diversity and the dependence on one plant turned the potato from hero to villain and the rest is history. Today, potatoes are commercially grown under a regimen of pesticides and herbicides to insure the public of a perfect white product, some even genetically engineered to kill any insect fool enough to take a bite. Most commercial potatoes are treated so they will not sprout which is why, if you wish to grow your own, you need seed potatoes. They are not treated. Potatoes don't even need a garden, they can be grown in a bale of hay. Place the bale on its side, cut side up. Slice up the seed potatoes with an eye in each piece and stuff the pieces about half way down and wet down the bale. Keep watering and the plant will grow and prosper until you break open the bale and retrieve your potatoes.

BOXTY

Boxty on the griddle
Boxty in the pan
If you can't make boxty
You'll never get your man

Old Irish Rhyme

From the Gaelic word "bacstai" (grilled over fire) these potato cakes have many versions. They can be made into a small cakes or, with a thinner batter, produce one large boxty per person which can be folded omelet-style or rolled crepe-style and filled with meats and sauces of choice.

4 large potatoes
1 cup flour
1 t baking soda

1 cup milk
1 egg, slightly beaten
1 cup butter, melted
3 T chives, chopped
1 T parsley

Cut two unpeeled potatoes into sections and boil for 20 minutes or until soft. Drain and mash. Grate two peeled potatoes on the coarse side of a grater. Add them to the mashed potatoes with 1/2 cup of the flour, baking soda, 1/2 cup of the milk and egg. Stir well; the mixture will be very stiff. Add half the melted butter, the remaining 1/2 cup flour, and 1/2 cup milk. Mix until well combined. If the mixture seems too stiff, add a little more milk. If you wish to make thinner, crepe-like, boxty, the batter will need to be teven hinner; more to the consistency of pancake batter.

In a large nonstick skillet over medium-high heat, heat 1 T of butter. When it is hot, drop the batter by large spoonfuls into the pan. Using a spatula, shape the cakes so they are even rounds about 3 inches across. Don't crowd the pan. Cook for 4 minutes or until the undersides are brown. Turn and brown the other side for 3 minutes. Be sure they are cooked through so the raw potatoes is done which might mean adjusting the heat so that the outside does not cook too fast. If cooking crepe-like boxty, you can use a crepe pan. If you need to keep the boxty warm, transfer them to a rimmed baking sheet and keep them in a 275 degree oven.

STUFFED POTATOES

4 medium to large potatoes
½ cup scallions diced (try ¼ cup chives or ramps)
1 T butter
1 cup cottage cheese
3 t milk
1 cup grated cheese of choice (cheddar, pepper jack, monterey)

Scrub potatoes, pierce in several places and bake in a 375 degree pre-heated oven for 1 hour. While the potatoes are cooking, sauté the scallions in 1 T butter until tender. If using chives or ramps, sauté for 1 minute and then add 2 T water and cook gently until tender. The water will keep the chives or ramps from becoming too crispy. Slice the potatoes in half and scoop out as much soft potato as possible. In a large bowl, combine the potato with the cooked scallions, chives or ramps, cottage cheese and mix. Add the grated cheese. Spoon this mixture back into the potato skins, place in a baking dish and bake for another 20-30 minutes or until the cheese has melted. Serve hot.

MINT POTATO SALAD

4-6 potatoes
1 small clove of garlic, diced
2-3 stems of fresh mint or 1 T dried mint
½ cup sour cream or plain yogurt
½ cup mayonnaise
2 T oil
1 T hard apple cider

Scrub the potatoes and then dice them into bite-size cubes. In a large pot, cover with water and bring to a boil. Boil for about 10 minutes or until the potatoes are "al dente" or still have texture when you bite into them. While they are cooking, whisk together the oil, hard cider and garlic. Drain the potatoes and toss with the oil mixture while still hot. Allow to sit for 15 minutes and the hot potatoes will continue to cook a bit absorbing the garlic flavor. Cover and refrigerate. This step can be done a day ahead. When ready to serve, mix the mayonnaise, sour cream or yogurt and mint together and toss with the potatoes.

VERMONT MASTER GARDENER HELP LINE
1-800-639-2230

Help for the basics of:
     Starting seeds indoors
     Planning and planting a garden
     Testing your soil
     Identifying disease - tomato blight being one!
     Controlling invasives
     Dealing with insects and pests

master.gardener@uvm.edu
A service of the University of Vermont Extension

PUMPKIN

Early settlers used pumpkins in a wide variety of recipes from desserts to stews and soups. The origin of pumpkin pie is thought to have occurred when the colonists sliced off the pumpkin top, removed the seeds, and then filled it with milk, spices and honey. The pumpkin was then baked in the hot ashes of a dying fire. Not all pumpkins are equal. Canned pumpkin comes from a tan colored pumpkin variety that looks nothing like a pumpkin. Face or jack o'lantern pumpkins are OK to eat but probably won't have the flavor of a pie or sugar pumpkin.

PUMPKIN SOUP IN THE SHELL

1 cooking or pie pumpkin (see above)
Cut off the top, scoop out seeds and stringy parts and rub the inside flesh with salt. Set the pumpkin in an oven proof bowl large enough for space around the sides. Measure how much liquid the pumpkin will hold with a measuring cup and water. Pour out the water. From that measurement, use equal parts chicken or vegetable stock and milk to make the broth.
½ cup fresh sage leaves or 3 T dried leaves
3 garlic cloves roasted gently in the oven for 10 minutes until soft and mashed.
Combine the broth and all ingredients in a pot and heat carefully. Fill the pumpkin with the hot broth and replace the lid (place a sheet of foil in between to keep it from falling in). Bake at 375 degrees for 1-2 hours, scraping the sides of the pumpkin into the soup as it softens. You may have to puree the soup and return it to the pumpkin. With luck it can be served intact!

PUMPKIN SEEDS

Don't toss out those seeds! For great snacks these are hard to beat. Boil the seeds in salted water for roughly 10 minutes before draining and drying. Your seeds will have a nice crunch to them, and more balanced salt distribution. Additional flavoring can be added after drying - sweet - hot - experiment!

PREPARING PUMPKIN FOR PIES

There are several ways to cook the pumpkin and considering the size of your pumpkin, you might want to use all three! Regardless of the method you use, taste each pumpkin. Bland pumpkins might need more sugar if used for a pie or perhaps would be better for soup or stews. Sweet pumpkins might indicate using less sugar for a pie. To get a nice, smooth consistency, put the cooked pumpkin through a food processor or blender. Use fresh or pack 2 cups of the puree into a freezer bag and freeze for future use.

Microwave - Remove the stem, halve the pumpkin (you are going to need a big knife!) and remove the pulp and seeds. Keep the seeds! Halve again and put one or two pieces in a microwave safe dish, add a couple of inches of water, cover it, and put in the microwave. Use settings per your microwave or cook at medium power about 20-30 minutes. Pumpkins are dense and may cook on the top, but as you scoop out the pumpkin, you may find raw pulp closer to the skin. You will need to return that to the microwave and finish cooking it before scooping the rest out.

Oven – Follow the above instructions but put the pumpkin halves or quarters in a covered baking dish and cook in a preheated 350 degree oven for 30-40 minutes or until the pumpkin feels soft to the touch. Remove and scrape the cooked pumpkin from the skin.

Steam – Remove the stem, halve the pumpkin (big knife), remove the pulp and seeds. Use a peeler to remove the skin, You may want to quarter the pumpkin to make this easier. Cut the pumpkin into cubes and place in a large pot with a steamer basket inside it with boiling water under. Steam for 15-20 minutes or until easily pierced with a fork.

PUMPKIN PIE IN A PUMPKIN

One night I got creative and conjured up this dish. It was far more complicated than I imagined but when I served it to my neighbor, who claims that his mother is the ONLY one who can make a good pumpkin pie, he ate the whole thing. His wife immediately wanted the recipe as his mother was coming for Thanksgiving. Indeed a work of love but worth it.

1 small sugar or pie pumpkin

Preheat the oven to 350 degrees. Cut off the top of the pumpkin and remove all of the seeds and pulp. Place the pumpkin in an oven proof casserole dish (it will be served in this dish) and fill the pumpkin with hot water. Place in the oven and bake for 1 hour, scraping the sides as the pumpkin bakes. You may want to cover the top of the pumpkin with foil should it start to look too dark. Depending on the density of the pumpkin, it may take longer until the sides scrape off easily. Be careful not to scrape too much at the bottom of the pumpkin. When done, remove and pour off the water and pulp, reserving the water, into a strainer. Allow the pulp to drain for 10 minutes while preparing the filling. Refill the pumpkin with the strained hot water to keep the pumpkin hot and from collapsing.

You can simply make a single pie crust
and fill it with this same mixture.

1 1/2 cup evaporated milk or a substitute
1/4 cup brown sugar
1/2 cup sugar
1/2 t salt
1 t cinnamon
1/2 t ginger
1/4 t nutmeg or allspice
1/8 t cloves
2 eggs, beaten slightly

Take the strained pulp and put it through the food processor to make 2 cups of puree. If you do not get 2 cups, be prepared with additional puree made from another pumpkin. Mix the above ingredients with the pumpkin puree. Pour the hot water out of the pumpkin and pour in the pumpkin puree mix. Top the filled pumpkin with foil and return to the oven for 1 ½ hours or until the filling is firm to the touch. A shortcut here is to use a convection oven which will cut the time in half or to microwave the filled pumpkin for 10 minutes on medium before placing it in the oven. Serve the entire pumpkin in the casserole with a spoon to scoop out the filling. Whipped cream is suggested.

PUMPKIN AND SAGE SAUCE

1 cup heavy cream
½ cup pumpkin puree
1 clove minced garlic
1/3 cup fresh sage leaves or 2 T dried sage
Salt and pepper to taste
1 T butter

Gently sauté the garlic in the butter. On medium heat, add the cream, pumpkin and half of the sage. Simmer for 10-15 minutes until slightly thickened. Add salt and pepper to taste. Garnish with the remaining sage.

STUFFED PUMPKIN

The amount of ingredients used will depend on the size if your pumpkin. This is based on a 5 pound pumpkin but if you end up with more than what will fit, you can keep it aside and add it later to the meal. Cooking time can also vary due to the size of the pumpkin so plan ahead. The cooked pumpkin will keep nicely in a warm oven until ready to be served. You will be amazed at the amount of food that comes out of this dish as the cooked pumpkin, when scraped off of the sides, keeps adding and adding to the meal!

1 T butter
1 onion, chopped
3 cloves garlic or to taste
2 carrots
1 sweet potato
2-3 small to medium potatoes
1 cup chopped broccoli
2 cups vegetable or beef or chicken broth
1 cup diced meat of choice (beef, chicken or neither)
1 T butter
1 large sugar pumpkin, top removed, seeded
1 oven proof round casserole dish large enough for the pumpkin bottom.
2 cups sour cream
Parsley to garnish

Preheat the oven to 350 degrees. In a large skillet, melt the butter and sauté the garlic. Add the carrots, sweet potato and potato and cook until half done. Add the broccoli. Cover and cook all of the vegetables together for 2-3 minutes. You do not want to over cook. Remove into a large bowl. Cook the meat by searing it in butter but do not fully cook. Add to the vegetables and mix thoroughly. Place the pumpkin in the casserole dish. Now stuff the pumpkin and pour the stock over the vegetables and place in the oven to cook for 1 hour or until the sides of the pumpkin soften. This may take longer depending on the size if the pumpkin. As the pumpkin cooks, scrape the sides to add to the stuffing. You may want to cover the pumpkin with foil should it start to brown too much. The liquid will be absorbed and the sides of the pumpkin soft when done. The pumpkin can keep in a warm over for up to an hour before serving. Top with 1 cup sour cream and parsley. Serve with extra sour cream.

CARAMELIZED PUMPKIN SAUCE

2 cups cubed pumpkin, fresh or frozen
2 large onions
2 T butter
1/2 cup heavy cream
ungrated parmesan cheese
Pasta of choice, penne suggested

Cut the pumpkin and onion in very thin slices. If using frozen pumpkin cubes, cut when still half frozen In a heavy saucepan, sauté the onion in the butter over until soft but not brown, then add the chopped pumpkin, mix and cook for as long as it takes to get soft and brown and start to caralmelize, up to 20 minutes. This time will vary depending on fresh or frozen pumpkin cubes. Turn off the heat and add half a cup heavy cream. Cook the pasta al dente (2 minutes less than perfect), do not rinse. Place in a warm serving dish and toss with the sauce, the pasta will continue cooking in the dish. Grate the parmesan over the top and serve.

RHUBARB

By the time you have planted your peas, rhubarb is ready to pick. As thrilling as it is to finally get your hands on something fresh from the garden it is hard to come up with things to do with it, so , have pie for breakfast! Cut off the seed stem that will appear with amazing speed shortly after the plant leafs out. Pull any large leafed, thick stems to allow tender young stems to develop and you can have rhubarb all summer long.

Also see Rhubarb Delight - Vermont "lemonade"

RHUBARB PIE

20-30 young rhubarb stems
1 unbaked pie shell *(see Pie Crust Dough)*
1 cup flour
1 cup sugar
2 T butter
Topping
6 T butter
1/3 cup flour
½ cup sugar

Preheat the oven to 350 degrees. Remove the leaves, rise and cut stems into 2 inch pieces. Place in a large bowl and toss with the flour and sugar, adjusting sugar to taste. Heap the mixture into the prepare pie shell, it should form a mound about an inch above the plate as it will reduce with cooking. Dot with butter. Soften the remaining butter and mix with the flour and sugar to form a crumb topping. Sprinkle over the top of the mound. Bake for 45-60 minutes until it bubbles. Cool before serving.

RHUBARB CAKE

This is an easy and delightful breakfast treat or dessert but calls for the challenge of substituting Bisquick, a good exercise to demonstrate just how easy that is.

10 young rhubarb stems
1 ½ cups Bisquick or substitute
½ cup sugar
1/2 cup milk or water
2 T butter
1 egg

Preheat the oven to 350 degrees. Remove the leaves, rise and cut the stems into 2 inch pieces. Grease a 8" square or 9" round baking pan. In a large bowl, mix together all but the rhubarb to form a cake batter. Stir in the rhubarb and pour into the baking pan. Bake for 30-35 minutes or until a toothpick comes out clean.

ROSES

Roses in Vermont? Perhaps not tea roses, but the wild varieties of Rosa rugosa and Multiflora rose fair very well, blooming in June and again in September. Rose hips are the cherry-sized red fruits of the rose bush left behind after the bloom has died. The flavor is described as fruity and spicy, much like the cranberry. In World War I I, rose hips were the primary source of vitamin C and grown in Victory Gardens. They were not only made into syrup and jelly, but considered a dinner vegetable. Many historical recipes call for rose water for flavoring. You can make your own quite easily. Whatever you don't cook with, spray on your pillow for a lovely scent.

ROSE HIP JELLY

 Harvest the fruits after the first light frost when they become fully-colored to a brilliant cherry red, but not overripe or dry and wrinkled. They should yield to gentle pressure somewhat like a ripe cherry tomato. When cooking with rose hips, do not use any metal pans or utensils other than stainless steel or risk discoloration of the fruit and loss of its precious vitamin C stores. Be sure to remove all the seeds. They are covered with sliver-hairs that, when ingested, irritate the digestive system and cause what the indigenous people call "itchy bottom disease." Rose hips have very little natural pectin so a standard jelly recipe does not work, unless you want rose hip syrup?

4 cups rose hips with stem ends removed
3 cups water
Bring to a boil and simmer 1/2 hour. Strain through at least three layers of cheese cloth. It can drip overnight
You now have;
2 cups of rosehip juice (add up to 1/2 cup water if necessary)
3 1/2 cups sugar
6 - 7 t lemon juice (hard apple cider did not work as well)
1 pouch pectin

Simmer rose hips in water until soft, about 20-30 minutes. Crush to mash, and strain through a jelly bag or three layers of cheesecloth. Remember that warning about the seeds! Should make about 4 cups of rose hip juice.   Warning that this is a somewhat labor intensive task and best done with a good friend to keep cheering you on. Add to juice, lemon juice and pectin crystals and stir until mixture comes to a hard boil. Stir sugar in at once. Bring to a full rolling boil and boil for 1 minute, stirring constantly. Remove jelly from heat and skim off foam with metal spoon. Pour jelly into hot sterilized jars. The jelly has a wonderful flavor and is the consistency of liquid honey. However, the color will change from that lovely red to a more orange tone.

ROSE HIP TEA

Perhaps the most commonly known use of rose hips is to brew them into tea. For tea they may be used fresh or dried. To dry them, discard any with discoloration then rinse in cold water, pat dry, and spread on a wax paper-lined cookie sheet. It takes several weeks for them to dry. They will be darker in color, hard, and semi-wrinkly. Rub off any stems or remaining blossom ends. Pour them into jars for storage in a dark pantry or cupboard. For fresh brewing, steep 2-4 clean, i.e. seeded, hips in a cup of boiling water for about 10 minutes. Sweeten with honey and enjoy. To make a tea of dried hips, use only 2 hips to one cup of boiling water and steep for 10 to 15 minutes until they soften and release some of their pink color into the water, then smash with a spoon to release flavors. Strain the tea before drinking.

ROSE HIP TART

A traditional recipe of rose hips, dating at least to 1671, is rose hip tart. Preparation of the rose hips is a very time consuming task, but the result it well worth it. Who would expect roses to be such prolific seed producers? Remember that warning about the seeds! Preparation requires a sharp knife and a good long movie. It will take some time to develop a technique but one does get the hang of it eventually.

2 1/2 cups prepared fresh hips
3/4 cup water
2 T sugar,
1/2 t each ground cinnamon and ginger
Squeeze of lemon juice (not local, but in the historic recipe.
Can be substituted with hard apple cider.)
Pie crust for a small pie dish *(see Pie Crust Dough)*

Bring the rosehips to a boil, lower heat, and simmer for 15 minutes. Stir in sugar, spices, and lemon juice. I confess to using the juice to keep recipe true. Stir and simmer for another 5 minutes; set aside. Prepare pie crust, add the rose hip filling, then cover with remaining pastry. Seal the edges and pierce the top. Bake in a 375 degree oven for 25 minutes, or until golden. Remove from the oven, sprinkle the top with sugar, and return to the oven for another 5 minutes. Eat hot or cold with ice cream or whipped cream. Divine!

ROSE WATER

Rose water has a very distinctive flavor and is used heavily in Asian, and Middle East cuisine, especially in sweets. Some of Vermont cooking is from Lebanese origin. Classically, rose water is made using Damask roses, not native, so select local roses when they are the most fragrant.

2-3 quarts fresh rose petals
Water
Ice cubes or crushed ice

In the center of a large pot (a large canning pot is ideal) with an inverted lid (a rounded lid), place a fireplace brick. On top of the brick place the bowl. Put the roses in the pot; add enough flowers to reach the top of the brick. Pour in just enough water to cover the roses. The water should be just above the top of the brick. Place the lid upside down on the pot. Turn on the stove and bring the water to a rolling boil, then lower heat to a slow steady simmer. As soon as the water begins to boil, toss a bag of ice on top of the lid. Use a turkey baster to remove the water as the ice melts. As the water boils the steam rises, hits the top of the cold lid, and condenses. As it condenses it flows to the center of the lid and drops into the bowl. However, if you simmer the water too long, you will continue to produce distilled water but the rose essence will become diluted and lose its smell. Remove the distillate with your turkey baster every 10 minutes and sniff and taste. It's time to stop when you start losing the smell and taste of roses.

LAVENDER COOKIES WITH ROSE WATER ICING & FLOWERS

½ cup butter
1 cup sugar
2 eggs
1 t lavender, crushed
1 ½ cups flour
2 t baking powder
¼ t salt

For Icing
2 cups powdered sugar
6 ½ t rose water

Preheat oven to 375 degrees. Cream together the butter and sugar. Add the eggs, lavender, flour, baking powder and salt. Drop by teaspoons onto an ungreased cookie sheet to make small, bite size, cookies. Bake for about 10 minutes. While the cookies bake, prepare the icing by mixing the powdered sugar with rose water. If edible flowers are in season, such as violets, lilacs(yes, they are edible) , johnny pop-ups or borage, place a flower in a drop of icing and let it set up. Lovely served fresh or you can allow the flower to dry in the icing.

Vermont Localvore Organizations

Upper Valley Localvores – www.uvlocalvore.com
Addison County Localvores – www.acornvt.org/localvore.html
Central Vermont Localvores – http:contralvtlocalvores.pbwiki.com
Champlain Valley Eat Local – www.eatlocalvt.org
Keene Localvores – www.hannahgrimes.come/localvore
Mad River Localvores –www.vermontlocalvore.org
Northeast Kingdon Localvores – village_greens@yahoo.com
Post Oil Solutions (Brattleboro) – www.postoilsolutions.org
Rutland Area Localvores – skyobrien.googlepages.com/localvores
Springfield Localvores – sharonm@vermontel.net
West Brookfield Locavores – anita@innevi.com

SQUASH

The term "winter squash" dates back to a time when the seasons were more crucial to man's survival than they are now. "Good keepers" became known as winter vegetables if they would "keep" until December. Winter squash take a longer time to mature and are harder skinned than summer squash and come in many varieties. Most can be switched in any recipe calling for a winter squash.

Acorn – green and shaped like an acorn, very common and tasty.

Ambercup – looks like small pumpkin.

Banana – yellow and long like a banana and can grow up to 2 feet.

Butternut – tan and shaped like a vase, very common and tasty.

Butter cup – green and shaped like a turban. The sweetest of all varieties.

Carnival – half green and half yellow with spots and a ribbed skin.

Delicata – a heirloom squash, yellow with green ribs with an elongated shape.

Hubbard – greenish grey, this is the largest and most irregular shaped squash.

Kabocha – Japanese it resembles a green pumpkin.

Spaghetti – yellow, oval and smooth skinned, named after its stringy flesh.

Sweet Dumpling – small, cream with green ribs and a dented in top

STUFFED SQUASH BLOSSOMS

Before your squash matures, you can enjoy this delightful dish from the blossoms. It makes no difference where the squash blossoms come from, but pumpkins and gourds have large and plentiful ones and will go until frost. (Note: if you want to eat your pumpkins, do not plant gourds anywhere near them as they will cross pollinate). Blossoms are best picked during the day when open and fresh. If they close, check carefully for a trapped bee inside or your preparation might get a little exciting!

8-12 blossoms
4 oz. goat cheese or cream cheese
½ cup fresh basil, chopped or torn
1 T Hard apple cider
½ cup oil
¼ cup balsamic vinegar (any substitute is not the same)

Warm the cheese to the point it is easy to mix. Add half of the basil and apple cider and mix. Remove the stems from the blossoms and fill with a spoonful of cheese mix. In a baking dish, combine the oil and vinegar and stir until smooth. Place the stuffed blossoms in the dish and cover with plastic wrap. Microwave gently for 3-6 minutes or until the dish is steaming. A fabulous appetizer.

BAKED SQUASH

Winter squash is delicious simply baked and with the many varieties available, will distinguish themselves in taste, some being sweet, some being nutty. To enhance these tastes, experiment with seasonings. You will, however, discover why some varieties were considered "good keepers" as your attempts to cut through their

hard shell might have you reaching for a chain saw! The hubbard is particularly challenging.

Depending on the size of the squash, halve or quarter it. If you can halve it, place it cut side down in a baking dish with enough water to cover the bottom of the dish up to ¼ inch. Cover and bake for 45 minutes to an hour depending on the size of the squash. It will be done when feeling soft to your touch. You can microwave, following your models instructions, in half the time.

Serve as is – winter squash is very attractive served in its shell. You can add apples and celery sauted in butter or bread crumb stuffing with onions, celery, fresh sage and maple syrup or come up with your own filling, be creative. Bake the stuffed squash another 15 minutes and serve warm.

Mash it– The cooked flesh can be scooped out and mashed. You can add milk or cream, maple syrup, honey or sage. Keep tasting as each squash has its own flavor that you will want to enhance with your seasoning. Spaghetti squash can be scooped out and sautéed in oil, adding chopped garlic and a grated light, dry cheese such as made from raw milk, heated until melted. Serve hot.

Freeze it – if you have too much, just freeze it. Cooked squash can be frozen in cubes or pureed and will make wonderful soup at a later date.

SQUASH BISQUE – 3 WAYS

Just about any winter squash, including pumpkin, lends itself to soup but you may want to start with butternut squash as it is easy to peel and most commonly used in soup recipes. Or you can use frozen squash cubes or puree.

> 1 **squash, peeled, cubed (about 6 cups) or squash or choice**
> 2 T **butter**
> 1 **medium onion, chopped**
> 2 **stalks celery, chopped**
> 2 **medium potatoes, peeled**
> 6 **cups vegetable stock**
> 4 T **flour**
> 2 **bay leaves**
> 2 t **chopped fresh thyme or 1/2 t dried**

In a large sauce pan, saute the chopped onion and celery in the butter until translucent, about 5 minutes. Add squash, if fresh, and sauté until beginning to brown, about 10 minutes. If using thawed squash, do not add yet. Pour in the vegetable stock and add the potatoes. Mix the flour with a little of the hot liquid to make a paste and then add to the soup. Cook for 10 minutes and then add the squash. Season with the bay leaves and thyme and simmer for 20 minutes. Remove from the heat and allow to stand or refrigerate until needed. Standing time will improve the flavors. Remove the bay leaves before the next step.

Serve as a robust, chunky soup.

Puree into a smooth thick soup, placing a dollop of sour cream in each bowl.

Add cream to the puree for a rich, elegant soup, garnish with fresh thyme.

SWEET POTATOES

Although sweet potatoes are grown in Vermont, the slips come from elsewhere and need to be started inside before planting after the danger of frost. A slip is a single plant, with small roots, that is sprouted on the sweet potato root and then "slipped" off to plant in the garden to grow a sweet potato plant. You can do this yourself but you need to start the slips in March.

VERMONT MAPLE SWEET POTATOES

3 lb sweet potatoes
3 T butter, cut into small pieces
¼ cup maple syrup
¼ cup apple cider
Salt and pepper

Boil the whole potatoes until almost tender when pierced, about 20 minutes. Drain and let cool enough to handle. While they are boiling, combined the maple syrup and cider in a small pan and bring to a simmer. Allow the mixture to reduce for about 4-5 minutes being careful that it does not froth up over the pan. Preheat the oven to 350 degrees and butter a 13 x 9 inch glass baking dish. Now that the potatoes are cool, peel them and cut lengthwise into quarters. Layer in the baking dish, seasoning each layer with salt and pepper, dots of butter and the maple syrup/cider mixture. To the top layer with butter. Cover tightly and bake 45 minutes to an hour until well glazed and very soft.

SWEET POTATO PANCAKES

1 cup grated raw sweet potato
1 cup grated raw white potato
1 cup grated carrot
2 T grated onion
1 small clove garlic, grated
¼ cup parsley
4 eggs, slightly beaten
1/3 cup flour
1 stick butter

Salt and pepper
Topping - apple sauce, plain yogurt or sour cream

If you can get someone to grate everything for you, do it. Otherwise plan for a 10 minute break after you are done grating, you will need it. Combine all of the ingredients into a large bowl and mix thoroughly. In a large skillet, melt the butter and dollop a large spoonful of the batter into the butter, flattening it with a spoon. Smaller pancakes cook better than large fat ones, but experimentation will find the right size. Do not turn too early, the pancake should be brown and crispy when done. Use a flat spatula to remove the cooked pancakes onto a plate and keep warm while cooking the rest. This recipe will make a pretty good pile of pancakes and they can be reheated in the microwave or oven before serving. Top with homemade applesauce, plain yogurt or sour cream.

TOMATOES

If you are going to go through the effort of growing your own tomatoes, don't just settle for the same product offered in the grocery stores. Expand your knowledge of tomatoes by discovering some of the great heirloom varieties such as "yellow out-red in". Developed for taste, not storage capacity, these tomatoes will raise the bar in taste and texture. Vermont, being in Zone 5, presents a challenge for growing tomatoes. August brings the first one to the plate and every meal should contain these delicious darlings until first frost. Unfortunately in Vermont, that could be September. If you start them from seed, which many of the heirlooms are only available as, March winds will be whipping snow past the window when you set out your seedlings under lights. You can harden them on a porch in May, but fight back the temptation to plant in the garden before Memorial Day, Vermont cannot be trusted. If you choose to purchase plants, the same rule applies...even more so if they came out of a greenhouse. Harden the plants for a week and then put the plants into the soil half of their height, i.e., deep. Another trick is to help warm the soil by placing green gallon size glass wine jugs filled with water around the plants. Solar energy warms the water during the day which transmits that heat back into the soil at night. This is Zone 5, you need to cheat a little and the comments about your drinking habits will be worth it. Vermont also offers hot house grown tomatoes for the nine months there are none in the garden. Not as good as the real thing, but vastly better than those shipped from California or Florida.

TOMATO/BASIL SANDWICH

Bread
Sliced tomato, fresh from the garden
Basil
Mayonnaise

Put the sandwich together, tearing the basil to release the flavor. Delicious!

TOMATO SAUCE

Tomato sauce is endlessly forgiving. It can be made thicker, thinner, saltier, sweeter, milder, or more complex to suit any occasion and any palate. It has endless uses and can be canned or frozen and taste as good as the day it was made. All I know is what I learned at my best friend's family Italian restaurant. Her mother was from Italy, I could barely understand her at times, but it was clear that every time she walked past the pot of simmering sauce on the stove, she would taste it, add something, and walk away. Average time on the stove was a day and a half and the sauce was amazing.

There are three basic styles of sauces: Long, short and raw.

LONG SIMMERING

10 ripe tomatoes (plum tomatoes have more pulp, less water but any tomato will do)

2 T olive oil

2 T butter

1 onion, chopped

1 pepper, chopped

2 carrots, chopped

2 stalks celery, chopped

4 cloves garlic, diced

¼ cup fresh basil or 3 T dried basil

1/8 cup fresh oregano or 1 T dried oregano

¼ cup red wine, the fuller flavored the better

The hardest part of making homemade sauce is peeling the tomatoes! You can use the traditional method of plunging the tomatoes into boiling water and then dropping them into iced water, but you will lose nutrients and flavor and make the tomato mushy. The tomato should never spend more than 10 seconds in the hot water and be allowed to cool on its own. Rubbing the skin with the dull side of a knife will loosen the skin before peeling with a knife. Plum tomatoes skins come off pretty easy with a vegetable peeler. Tomatoes can be frozen whole, just wash, place on a cookie sheet and pop in the freezer. Once frozen, place in freezer bags and keep until needed. When thawed, the skins just slide off so you get right down to making sauce. Chop 8 of the peeled tomatoes and puree. Reserve 2 and set aside. In a large pot cook onion, bell pepper, carrot, celery and garlic in oil and butter until onion starts to soften, about 5 minutes. Pour in pureed tomatoes. Stir in chopped tomato, basil, Italian seasoning and wine. Bring to a boil, then reduce heat to low, cover and simmer 2 hours. Taste, adjust seasoning and simmer an additional 2 hours. Taste again, adjust again and simmer until you have the flavor you want.

BARELY-COOKED SAUCE has a flavor more like fresh tomatoes, but the cooking softens the tomatoes and blends the flavors.

6 tomatoes, peeled and chopped
¼ cup olive oil
3 onions, minced
2 peppers, minced
4 cloves garlic, minced
3 T white wine
Salt
Pepper

In a large saucepan, heat the oil and add all of the ingredients. Cover and simmer for 30 minutes. Serve.

RAW – Select tomatoes at their peak of ripeness. Quarter and seed the tomatoes, but you don't have to skin them. Chop them into fine pieces or grate them which will produce a smoother, juicier sauce. Combine with fresh herbs, such as basil, oregano and parsley, toss with olive oil and salt and pepper. If you let the sauce sit for a few hours it will enhance the flavors.

COUNTRY FRESH TOMATO SOUP

Fresh or frozen tomatoes can be used for this recipe with equal success.

1 quart fresh tomatoes
2 cups calcium enriched water*
1 small onion, diced
5 whole cloves of garlic
¼ t powdered ginger
1 t salt
1 t sugar
¼ t baking soda to reduce acid
2 T butter
2 T flour

Cook for 20 minutes; strain, re-heat. Melt the butter, add flour and the hot strained liquid, stir together. Serve hot or cold.
calcium enriched water: Boil eggs for 5 minutes, let stand in the hot water for 5 more minutes. Use slotted spoon to remove eggs. Strain water, the eggs have leached the calcium into the boiling water.
From the kitchen of Linda K. Schneider

Also see: Fiddlehead Tomato Salad
Artesian grilled cheese sandwich

TURKEY

Of the 400 million turkeys raised in America, 99% are Broad-Breasted Whites. Heirloom turkeys, such as the Jersey Bluff, Black Spanish, Beltsville Small White, Standard Bronze, Narragansett, Royal Palm, Midget White and Bourbon Red have increased in popularity and are available in Vermont and offer a variety of tastes. If you want such a turkey, reserve one with a grower as they go fast. My neighbor received a turkey from an employee who raised them for the first time. In his enthusiasm, he started early and gave those turkeys everything they could want for. The result was a 42 pound dressed bird that arrived Thanksgiving morning in her kitchen but couldn't possibly fit in the oven. At a loss of what to do, she called the local radio station running a Thanksgiving Day help show, where they, after a good laugh, instructed her to halve the bird and cook part in the oven and part on the BBQ. She said it was the best turkey she ever had.

VERMONT GLAZED TURKEY
1 fresh turkey
1 cup maple syrup
2 T mustard
1 cup onions, finely chopped
1 medium shallot, finely chopped
¾ lb. bacon or turkey bacon
2 T butter
1 cup turkey broth (from the baked turkey)

While the turkey is cooking, cook the bacon, pouring off most of the fat, (turkey bacon will not produce much fat but pork bacon will), and reserve. Saute the onion and shallot in the butter, add the mustard, broth and maple syrup and cook until it thickens into a glaze. Mix in the bacon. 30 minutes before the turkey is to be done, pour the glaze over the top of the bird.
From the kitchen of Eileen R. Growald

POACHED TURKEY BREASTS IN WINE
4 turkey fillets, sliced thin
¼ cup onion, diced
2 T fresh tarragon or 1 T dried tarragon
¾ - 1 cup white wine

4T flour
1 T parsley
1 T hard apple cider

Poach the turkey fillets in the wine with the onion and half of the tarragon. The fillets should float in the wine, if not, add more. Remove and keep warm. Boil the wine mixture down half. Combine the flour with a small amount of hot liquid and then add to the broth. Add the rest of the tarragon and cook until thickened, about 2 minutes. Stir in the hard apple cider. Pour the sauce over the tenderloins. Excellent served over fresh spinach or chilled and used for a sandwich.

COOKING A WILD TURKEY

In 1621, at the first Thanksgiving, wild turkey was served. Aside from one short letter from Edward Winslow, there is no other account, *"our Govenour sent foure men on fowling, that so we might after a more speciall manner rejoice together, after we had gathered the fruit of our labors, they foure in one day killed as much fowle, as with a little helpe beside, served the Company almost a weeke."* If you really want a traditional Thanksgiving, cook a wild turkey. The only way you are going to get to cook a wild turkey is to barter for one. Unless you fancy yourself dressed up in camouflage gear, hiking out into the woods at 5AM and sitting perfectly still for hours until some dumb tom is convinced that the wooden turkey call you have been working for the past four hours in order to keep from freezing to death is really a hen turkey looking for some action. And even then, you will need the composure to move ever so slowly to sight the gun and squeeze the trigger even though your nose itches so badly that suppressing the sneeze is putting your blood pressure into the red zone not to mention the need to respond to nature after having three cups of coffee. But never mind, this is fun. The barter is not going to come cheap.

Skip plucking the bird, skin it instead.
Because the bird now has no skin, slather it with mayonnaise or wrap it in strips of bacon.
Bake in the oven just like any domestic turkey.
Don't even try to eat the drumsticks, this bird ran for a living.

VENISON

Come deer season in Vermont, everything stops. If you are having a roof put on your house, forget it until everyone gets their deer. This is part of that Vermont lifestyle you bought into when you moved here. When one factors in the cost of the license, the gun, the gear and the two weeks of missed work, venison is a very expensive meat. Best to barter for it. If you have enough land, tell the guys that you would like a flank or roast in return for hunting privileges. They will be most happy to oblige as a big buck takes up a lot of freezer space. At the very least, become buddies with a deer hunter and sooner or later you will be offered up some venison. Or buy a license. I had a friend whose wife picked off two deer in a row, first with the pick up truck then with the family car. Needless to say, this caused stress in the marriage, not so much over the totaled vehicles, rather that she was putting more venison in the freezer than he was. Unfortunately, this is not a very economical method to obtain venison, mostly because bruised meat is not fit to eat. He finally got a trophy buck and all was forgiven. This is when you begin to understand the Vermont lifestyle thing. If all else fails, you can seek out "game dinners" sponsored by hunting clubs throughout Vermont. Venison, moose and bear are the usual fare.

VENISON TENDERLOIN

The prime cut of meat from a deer, this deserves to be treated as such. My blacksmith, and long time woodsman, offers his favorite method of cooking.

Slice the tenderloin in to ½ - ¾ inch fillets or butterfly them.

Using an entire stick of butter, sauté the fillets until just done and serve.

From the kitchen of Bruce Hickey

BAMBI'S VENISON STEW

This recipe comes from Bambi, my neighbor, not Bambi, the fawn. "Women deer hunters were not that common when I first started hunting 30 years ago. Imagine the look on the clerk's face when I checked in my first deer and he looked at the name on the license!" She figured that everyone should be famous for some dish and since her name was Bambi, well, it was obvious to her what it should be.

Bambi admits to not really having a recipe, but a feel for the stew, and encourages you to experiment. Just don't add tomatoes, they overpower the dish.

1 lb ground venison
2 onions, chopped
2 whole bay leaves
2 cups corn
2 cups green beans (other vegetables of choice can be substituted)
4 medium potatoes, diced with the skin on
Water or sauterne wine
Juniper berries (optional - but this is a great addition for any wild game. If you don't remove them at the end from the dish advise your guests so they can avoid eating the large berries as they are not tasty but impart great flavor)

Hunter spices
½ cup flour
2 t salt
1 t pepper
2 T fresh tarragon or 2 t dried tarragon
3 cloves of garlic, finely diced
1 shallot, finely diced or 3-4 ramps, finely diced

Brown ground venison slowly in pan keeping it from burning. Depending on how lean the venison is, you may have to add some butter to the pan. While browning the venison add the diced onion so it gets a bit glazed and soft. Mix in the hunter spices with the meat and onion while browning. It is important to put the spices in now to give the venison its flavor. After browning transfer meat and onions to a soup pot, scraping the spices from the pan as you transfer. Slowly add water and vegetables – until it is thick but you can still stir it. More juice will generate as you cook the vegetables so don't add too much water initially – you can always add more at the end if it's too thick but this is a stew not a soup. Bring the mixture to a boil and then turn down and let simmer until the vegetables are soft but firm. Keep a close watch, stirring often, so it doesn't burn on the bottom. Remove bay leaves. Make this dish ahead of time and allow to sit in the refrigerator for a day if possible to let the seasoning flavor it well.

From the kitchen of Bambi Prigel

WEEDS TO EAT

When picking a gathered plant be sure to use a field guide
or consult someone familiar with the plant before eating

DANDELIONS

The bane of lawns, dandelion greens show up early in April and are delicious as a salad when they are young and tender. Pick before the flower bud emerges, which is darn quick after greens appear. Older leaves are quite bitter and tough.

Salad - dress with maple syrup dressing to add sweetness.

Steamed - Steam lightly, 2 minutes or less and season to taste.

Flowers - Dip in a light batter and fry for an interesting treat

LAMBS QUARTERS

A "weed" commonly found in gardens starting in June, it is also known as "goosefoot" due to the distinctive shape of the leaves. Offered in fancy New York restaurants, waiters love to inform diners that it is not part of a sheep!

Steamed - Cook as if spinach or chard, season to taste.

SORREL

This delicate green herb is common to most lawns and gardens and is also known as spinach dock. It has a distinctive shape and even more distinctive taste, often compared to a Kiwi fruit but could be said to be "lemony." I have been known to crawl about on the lawn tasting plants until I found the right one!

Salad - An excellent topping to any salad.

Hors'd'oeuvres - bread slices and cream cheese with sorrel on top

Sorrel Soup

A bunch of sorrel
1/3 cup onion, chopped
1-2 cups chicken or vegetable broth
2-3 T Flour

Saute the onions in butter until soft, add the sorrel and cook until tender. Puree. Make a roux in a soup pot and add the broth slowing until thickened. Add the puree, mix and heat. Serve hot.
From the kitchen of Eileen Growald

98

WILD LEEKS AKA RAMPS

*When gathering wild plants, please
ask for landowner permission first.*

The common wild leek also known the ramp, is an
intriguing addition to the table in early spring. First to send
green shoots to the surface in the spring, it is easily spotted in bunches
along streams and in wet soggy ground once you acquire an eye for it.
It looks very much like lily of the valley but shows up in April. Tear
off a leaf and take a sniff, the distinct odor of onion will tell for sure
that it is a ramp. The wet soggy ground will not give up the ramps
easily and take care when using a spade as to not damage the plants.
Ramps do not like being harvested and might take several years to
replenish. Care must be exercised in order for the bed to survive. The
season is April and May as the plant dies back once warm weather
arrives. But until then, ramps can add greatly to spring cuisine. Since
it shows up at the same time as Morels one can search and find both
in one outing. Traditional recipes are eggs with ramps, potatoes with
ramps, fish with ramps, soups, casseroles and potato dishes. We'd like
to think that ramps can rise to a higher level of cuisine than that.

A papery wrapper leaf (and some dirt) may surround the bulb and
should be pulled off as you would with scallions. There may also be
some roots which should be trimmed off along with their little button
attachment. Once trimmed and cleaned the entire plant is tender and
choice for eating. Do not trim the roots off if you wish to store them in
the refrigerator, place in a glass of water to keep them from drying out.
They can last up to a week that way. They also can be frozen whole.

RAMP PESTO

This is so outstanding that I allowed myself to use olive oil, pine nuts
and parmesan cheese. Its uses are endless.

Two fistfuls of freshly picked ramps, cleaned
1 cup of olive oil
1 cup of pine nuts or sunflower seeds
Freshly grated parmesan cheese
Parsley (frozen from the season before)

Place the ramps and the nuts in a food processor and turn on. While mixing, add the oil gradually. Scrape the sides to be sure everything is mixed. Add the grated cheese and parsley to taste. Both will help cut the pungent flavor of the ramps and the amount used will be determined by your taste or the dish the pesto is to be used for. On pasta, I suggest cutting the flavor quite a bit but for fish or lamb, add only a little cheese. Pesto can be frozen until ramp season rolls around again.

RAMP AND POTATO SOUP

4 to 6 slices bacon (optional)
4 cups chopped ramps (including green)
4 to 5 cups diced red potatoes
3 T flour
4 cups chicken or vegetable broth
1 cup heavy cream
Salt and pepper, to taste

In a large skillet fry bacon until crispy; set bacon aside. Add ramps and potatoes to the skillet; fry on medium-low heat until ramps are tender. Take care as ramps can crisp up very fast, you only want them cooked through. Sprinkle with flour; stir until flour is absorbed. Stir in broth; simmer until potatoes are tender. Stir in the cream and heat thoroughly. Add salt and pepper to taste.

Also see
Artesian grilled cheese sandwiches.

Seed Savers

The purpose of seed saving is to reserve heirloom seeds that have been passed down through families and communities for generations, but are at risk of disappearing because of the dominance of industrial agriculture, which has elimintaed much of the genetic diversity present in world agriculture. Vermont seed savers offer climate tested varities of vegetables otherwise not available to gardeners. Seeds may be found at local farmers markets or farm shows.
Examples:
Vermont Cranberry Bean
Yellow Out/Red In Tomato

ZUCCHINI

In late August and September there is a joke about that being the only time Vermonters ever lock their cars....to prevent others from ridding themselves of their gardens overflow of zucchini into the back seat. There simply are not enough recipes to keep up with this prolific squash so don't even pretend to try.

ZUCCHINI PIE

3 cups sliced zucchini
1 Cup Bisquick - Substitution: 1 cup mix = 1 cup flour, 1 1/2 t baking powder, 1/2 t salt, 1 T oil or melted butter.

1 small onion sliced
1 clove garlic, chopped
4 eggs
½ cup sunflower oil
½ cup parsley
¼ cup grated dry parmesan cheese (no substitute)
Salt and pepper to taste
Grated mozzarella cheese for topping

Mix all ingredients, add the zucchini last. Pour into a round pie plate and top with the mozzarella cheese. Bake at 350 for 35-45 minutes until brown on top and bubbling on the sides. Cool before serving but serve warm.

ZUCCHINI ON THE BBQ

1 medium to large (not huge) zucchini per 2 people
Butter
Seasoning of choice such as basil, oregano or dill

Cut the zucchini in half, lengthwise. If really long, cut in half. For quicker and easier BBQing, par-boil for 10-15 minutes depending on size or place face down in a baking dish with a little water and microwave on medium for 10 minutes. The zucchini should be partially soft but not cooked through. Melt the butter and mix with the seasoning of your choice and brush onto the zucchini. Place on the BBQ and check periodically so it does not burn. The zucchini will be soft and browned and you will be amazed how sweet and tender it tastes.

ZUCCHINI ROLLAND

This is a variation of a recipe that usually uses eggplant, but since zucchini is so much more available in Vermont gardens, I modified the recipe. It is a very elegant dish and great for parties or company. The best part is that it can be made a day ahead and also that it freezes well.

1 large zucchini
1 cup bread crumbs
4 eggs
2 cups ricotta cheese
½ cup mozzarella cheese, grated
1 T fresh basil or 2 t dried basil
1 T fresh oregano or 2 t dried oregano
Olive oil (preferred over a substitute)
2 cups tomato sauce

Carefully slice the zucchini longwise into ¼ to ½ inch pieces. A large zucchini should yield 8 – 10 slices. If you need more, grab another zucchini. Whisk 2 eggs with a little water in a low sided dish. In another similar dish, place the bread crumbs. Dip each zucchini slice in first the egg and then the bread crumbs until completely coated. In a large frying pan, large enough to hold the long slices of zucchini, cover the bottom with enough oil to allow the zucchini to float when placed in it. Bring to medium heat before placing a zucchini slice in it. If the slice is too long, it will not cook evenly and you will have to work the piece back and forth. If this is the case, get a larger pan. Cook each slice of zucchini until browned, about 2 minutes per side. Remove and drain on paper towels. Mix together 2 eggs, the ricotta and mozzarella cheeses and spices. Line a baking dish with ½ of the tomato sauce. With the cooked zucchini laying flat, dollop in several spoonfuls of the cheese mixture and roll up the slice, placing it open side down in the baking dish. Repeat until done. Sometimes I have pieces left over and I put them on a small dish in the same manner. Top with the remaining tomato sauce. At this point you can freeze the dish or keep it for a day in the refrigerator. When ready to bake, top with grated mozzarella cheese and bake in a 350 degree oven for an hour or until bubbly. This dish also microwaves well.

HUGE ZUCCHINI SOLUTION

What to do when the zucchini gets larger than your thigh!

1 large zucchini: 3 1/2 - 4 lbs
1/2 lb sweet Italian sausage
1 large green bell pepper coarsely chopped
1 medium yellow Spanish onion, coarsely chopped
4 oz goat cheese
2 oz gruyere cheese, grated
1 egg beaten
1 cup bread crumbs
2 T finely chopped oregano
2 T finely chopped parsley
Salt and pepper to taste
Greased 9x13" baking dish

Preheat oven to 375. Par boil zucchini for 10 minutes (if it won't fit into your pot whole, cut in half crosswise). Slice the parboiled zucchini in half lengthwise. Scoop out the pulp and seeds leaving approximately 1/4 inch to keep the shell standing. Discard the large seeds. Chop the rest of the zucchini pulp and set aside in a medium to large mixing bowl. Remove the sausage from casing and sauté for 30 seconds in a large skillet (or the pot you cooked the zucchini in), breaking it up. Add onions and peppers and sauté until onion is translucent about 3 minutes. Transfer the sausage, onion and peppers (do not drain fat) to the bowl with the zucchini and stir to combine. Stir in oregano, parsley, salt and pepper.
Stir in bread crumbs. Crumble goat cheese and add to mixture with Gruyere and egg. Stir. Fill zucchini boat shells with stuffing and arrange in baking dish.
Bake, uncovered for 25 minutes.
From the kitchen of Michelle Gama

SUGGESTED COOKBOOKS

Clan of the Hawk. <u>Native American Recipes by The Abenaki Clan of the Hawk.</u> Vermont. Clan of the Hawk. 2008.

Gibbons, Euell, <u>Stalking the Wild Asparagus</u>. New York. David McKay Company. 1962.

Katzen, Mollie, <u>Moosewood Cookbook</u>. Ten Speed Press, CA. 1977

Kent, Louise Andrews. <u>The Vermont Year Round Cookbook</u>. Vermont. The Riverside Press. 1965.

Kingsolver, Barbara, <u>Animal, Vegetable, Miracle</u>. New York. Harper Perennial. 2007

Kreuter, Marie-Luise. <u>The Macmillan Book of Natural Herb Gardening</u>. New York. Macmillian Publishing Company. 1985.

Krumm, Bob. <u>The New England Berry Book</u>. Maine. Yankee Books. 1990.

Mann, Rick. <u>Backyard Sugarin'</u>. Vermont. Countryman Press. 1991.

Miller, Bill. <u>NAHC Wild Game Cookbook</u>. Minnesota. North American Hunting Club. 1991.

Underwood, Greer. <u>Gourmet Light</u>. Connecticut. The Globe Pequot Press. 1985.

White, Jasper. <u>Jasper White's Cooking From New England</u>. New York. Harper and Row. 1989.

SUGGESTED READING

Lloyd, John. Mitchinson, John. <u>The Book of Animal Ignorance</u>. New York. Harmony Books. 2007

Megyesi, Jennifer. <u>The Joy of Keeping Chickens,</u> New York. Skyhorse Publishing. 2009. ***Vermont author!***

Kurlansky, Mark, <u>The Food of a Younger Land</u>, Penquin Group, 2009

Pollan, Micheal. <u>The Botany of Desire</u>. New York. Random House. 2002

Pollan, Micheal, <u>The Omnivores Dilemma</u>, Penguin Press, 2006

Schlosser, Eric, <u>Fast Food Nation:The Dark Side of the All American Meal</u>, Houghton Mifflin Harcourt, 2001

BRING VERMONT INDOORS

VERMONT FEATHER TREE

Cut a relatively straight birch branch between 2 and 3 feet tall. Use a clay pot and secure the branch with quick cement. Once set, drill holes, slightly downwards, big enough to insert pine sprigs to resemble a pine tree. Do this in one dimension (holes opposite of each other, slightly staggered, all the way up the tree). Also drill a hole in the top. Insert pine sprigs, increasing the size as you go down the tree. Some experimentation will be needed to get the look you want. Hand cut figurines from scrap paper, dried apples, birch bark, dried flowers, pine cones, etc.

DRIED FLOWER ARRANGEMENTS

Hydrangea, Echinacea and oregano provide wonderful late summer flowers that dry very easily. Allow the flower to develop as much pinkish/rose color as possible but not allow it to get frosted, which requires daily vigilence of the weather from mid-September on. Hang and dry before using.

YULE LOG

Cut a length of birch log to the appropriate size for a fireplace, then halve it lengthwise so it sits flat. Drill in holes and stick freshly cut white pine sprigs all about. Use bailing twine from hay bales to tie up groups of pine cones and attach them in an artistic manner.

CANDLE HOLDER

Select a straight and blemish free small birch log about 4-6 inches in diameter and 12 inches long. Halve it lengthwise. Drill three 7/8 inch holes into which you will insert candles.

WILD DOGWOOD

The smooth red twig or red osier dogwood grows wild in Vermont. The long branches sprout lime green leaves and eventually a small cluster of white flowers. If you want the "tree" bloomed for Christmas, collect and start the branches just after Thanksgiving. We keep the "tree" all winter and plant it in the spring.

SUBSTITUTES

Substitutes will always produce slightly different results.

CORNSTARCH – 2 T flour for 1 T cornstarch.

EVAPORATED MILK – There several possible substitutions and each needs taste and texture to be kept in mind. Dry non-fat milk can be reconstituted using 40% of the water recommended. However, being non-fat milk, it might lack in flavor and texture in which case, combine with cream until you get the desired amount. Substituting with just cream might not give the right texture. Buttermilk has the texture but will effect taste as it is on the sour side. Or, you can reduce whole milk by simmering, not boiling, to 40% of its volume.

LEMON JUICE - Hard apple cider - Hard cider is acidic and dry and whisks well with oil. I prefer using naturally fermented hard cider without added sugar. The alcohol level is very low about 2%. If using bottled hard cider, the alcohol can be cooked off if desired.

MOLASSES – Made from boiling cane sugar and certainly was a commonly used ingredient by early settlers. One cup of molasses can be substituted with one cup of dark maple syrup or 1 cup of honey. "End of the run" maple syrup, which is very dark with a slight bitter aftertaste, can be a suitable substitute. We made it by mistake one year and now we have requests for it for baked beans.

OIL, VEGETABLE OR OLIVE - Sunflower oil has a distinct taste and may or may not be a suitable substitute in some recipes.

OIL IN BAKED GOODS - Applesauce – A very common substitute to reduce calories in baking. Use ½ the amount of unsweetened applesauce for the called on amount of oil in pancakes, muffins and cakes.

ORANGE JUICE – Sweet cider – Acidic and sweet this substitute will impart a different, but interesting, flavor.

RICE - Wheat berries – Vermont grown and very tasty, wheat berries are the seed kernel of wheat, however Vermont does have a rice grower, although still in fledgling status.

RAISINS - Currents – Currants come from sturdy bushes and are seasonal from June through August with some Vermont growers offering "pick your own." Dried currants are also available and are a very good substitute for raisins.

SHORTENING – Butter -1 cup butter for 1 cup shortening. For baked goods, add 1 T water or milk per ½ cup butter. Oil cannot be used as a substitute for baked goods calling for a solid shortening.

SUGAR - Maple syrup - ¾ cup maple syrup = 1 cup of white sugar
Mix the syrup with the liquid in the recipe, not the dry ingredients. If the recipe calls for butter or shortening, melt it and mix with the maple syrup. You may want to add ¼ to ½ t baking soda to neutralize the syrup's slight acidity unless the recipe uses yogurt, buttermilk or sour cream The distinct taste of maple sugar may or may not be suitable in some recipes.

or

Honey – use equal amounts up to one cup, then use 2/3 cup honey for each cup sugar. Reduce the baking temperature by 25 degrees as products with honey will brown faster. In baked goods, add ¼ t baking soda per cup of honey to reduce acidity.

or

Maple sugar – Maple sugar can be made by following the directions for making maple sugar candy, but use less syrup. It should be stored in a tightly sealed jar and will last indefinitely. It is outstanding in some recipes and too rich in others so experimenting is necessary. It is also available in stores.

TOMATO PASTE - 2-3 T of tomato puree or sauce, boiled down for 1 T tomato paste

VANILLA – equal or less amount of apple brandy depending on how strong a taste you want from it.

EATABLE DATEBOOK

MARCH -   Maple syrup

APRIL -
- Wild Leeks (Ramps)
- Dandelion Greens
- Fiddleheads
- Rhubarb

MAY -   Japanese Knotweed

JUNE -
- Strawberries
- Peas
- Roses
- Lamb's Quarters
- Grape leaves

JULY -
- Green beans
- Beet greens
- Sorrel
- Red & Black raspberries

AUGUST -
- Squash blossoms
- New Potatoes
- Cucumbers
- Early apples
- Blackberries
- Tomatoes
- Zucchini
- Peaches
- Corn
- Garlic

SEPTEMBER -   Pears, Plums, Apricots, Apples

OCTOBER -
- Concord grapes
- Thimble berries
- Sweet potatoes
- Pumpkins
- Rose hips
- Carrots
- Squash
- Beets

NOVEMBER -
- Potatoes
- Venison